Plumb Lines and Fruit Baskets

Sixteen timely, provocative
sermons on the prophets

Ralph L. Murray

BROADMAN PRESS • *Nashville, Tennessee*

© 1966 • BROADMAN PRESS
Nashville, Tennessee
422-296

DEWEY DECIMAL CLASSIFICATION NUMBER: 224
Library of Congress Catalog Card Number: 66-15145
Printed in the United States of America
5.N6513

*to my
mother and father
who first taught me
the meaning of faith*

Plumb Lines and Fruit Baskets

By Way of Interpretation

No one could seriously make the charge that prophetic preaching was "about questions no one was asking." Those who heard the prophets may well have wished to avoid the questions they were asking; they could not complain that the questions were ungermane. Just the contrary was true. The prophets were relevant, timely, and sometimes racy. To gain and hold attention they searched their imaginations. They gleaned truths from common life and set those truths walking before their hearers in arresting and graphic style. Their genius is best caught in the parables they told, the metaphors they used, the dramatic devices they employed. The prophets were anything but liturgical.

The truth they spoke had its immediate application, of course, but it also has a certain timeless quality. It was good for those who first heard it; it is good for us, too.

The chapters of this book are, quite frankly, homiletical in nature. The material was first developed as sermons—sermons *based on* sermons first preached by the prophets. It would be too much to claim that these pages rise to the height of their inspiration. They do not. But it is not too much to claim a robust faith in the method the prophets employed. If preaching is to reach the heart, it must be about things that concern the heart.

And if we can somehow catch the ear, we may reach the heart and plant there the truth God seeks to bring to those who know him not.

So, taking a cue from the prophets and following their methods only imperfectly, we set the plumb line over against our lives and our times; we examine carefully the values we cherish, lest they be nothing more than a basket of spoiled summer fruit.

Acknowledgements

The telephone rang. It was an invitation to teach a course in the School of Religion at the University of Tennessee here in our city. I accepted, and those winter quarter students and I began a study of the Old Testament prophets that was to continue, by fits and starts, for the next three years.

I later learned that the invitation had been made at the recommendation of my esteemed friend, Dr. Charles Trentham, pastor of Knoxville's First Baptist Church and Dean of the School of Religion. I am deeply grateful to him for that opportunity, for out of those three years of study came the material that fills this book.

I also want to acknowledge the expert assistance of Mrs. James Coram, who burned the candle low many a night to bring rough-hewn material into manuscript form.

There are other debts. Some I am aware of, some I am not. May I simply express the hope that what my creditors meet of themselves here will help convince them that they have not labored in vain.

Ralph L. Murray
November 12, 1965

Contents

1

Plumb Lines and Fruit Baskets

Amos 7:7-17; 8:1-3

Amos peered through the roseate glow of his times and saw what others could not: that Death and Eternity sat glaring at them. It was Israel's golden era. Jereboam II ruled a land that reveled in unparalleled prosperity. To the south was Judah, Amos' native land, where Uzziah reigned in unchallenged luxury and in undisturbed peace. In both Israel and Judah a mood of optimism and religious indifference prevailed. Danger seemed far off. Pride, fulness of bread, and famine of the spirit were the hallmarks of Amos' day.

But Amos saw beyond the apparent to the real. He sensed the approaching calamity. History bore him out. Within a generation Israel would be gone, fallen into the dust, never to rise again. And while all the external evidence seemed to run in a contrary direction, Amos spoke the conviction of his soul. He saw; he felt; and who could but prophesy?

In such a day, to such a mood, Amos came with his symbol of the plumb line and the basket of summer fruit.

When we reflect upon these two metaphors, it dawns on us that the plumb line is Amos himself. Here we are confronted with *preaching as a function*. The basket of summer fruit is the *message* Amos preached, the focus of the preacher's function.

1

In these two figures of speech, we discover Amos and his message.

As Amos confronts us, striding briefly upon the stage of holy history, we are face to face with more than this strange desert man. What audacity is this, that a man would dare to raise his voice in protest, claiming to hear the beat of another drummer?

The Function of Preaching

Here is a man—an ordinary man, at that—who cries out against the venality, the sanctioned immorality, the popular profanities, and claims his message is from the Lord. Here is a preacher who pits himself against the trend of the times. If we have half a mind, we must ask ourselves the obvious question: What is this thing called preaching? Is Amos a good example of the self-induced hypnosis that cloaks a man with an imagined but unreal authority?

These are questions for our time, too. How is preaching related to Christianity? What of liturgy (which someone has called "smells and bells") of which we have seen aplenty in television and movie? What of us nonliturgical people who dare to elevate one among us, designate him as preacher, and then gather to hear him declare the "word of the Lord"? Which is more faithful to the heart of things: the plain preacher with the Bible in his hand, or the robed priest with miter and scepter, scattering holy water as he proceeds through his mysterious and elaborate rites?

Will a lion roar in the forest, when he hath no prey? will a young lion cry out of his den, if he have taken nothing? Can a bird fall in a snare, . . . where no gin is for him? . . . Shall a trumpet be blown in the city, and the people not be afraid? shall there be evil in a city, and the Lord hath not done it? . . .

The lion hath roared, who will not fear? the Lord hath spoken, who can but prophesy? (3:4-8).

Clearly, Amos saw the preacher as one who must be faithful to himself and to the truth that he perceives. The preacher is nothing if not an honest man. He may have eloquence; he may have courage; but most of all he must have integrity.

More than the preacher is called into question; preaching itself is under review. What is preaching?

If Amos can make a contribution to the present dilemma, it would be in the area of defining preaching. For him, preaching was nothing more than calling attention to the overlooked, pointing out the inescapable, giving focus to the truth.

History teaches us that the free pulpit is the means by which the church judges herself. When the church had fallen on evil days, into the moral morass of the Dark Ages, she found her way to the light through the preaching of the word. The leaders of the Reformation threw off the yoke of the popes and the prelates, mounted their pulpits armed only with their Bibles, and declared to the people the word of God. The Bible was translated into the language people spoke; the truth of the Bible was set to music; the "smells and the bells" were exchanged for hymns people could sing and preaching they could respond to. For us of the evangelical tradition, the altar of the mass which celebrates a dead Christ is edged out by a preaching pulpit which declares a living Lord.

In November, 1963, Billy Graham spoke to the students and faculty at Princeton Seminary. Mr. Graham declared that today the church finds herself in a world revolution, that the church is beginning to lose power over the conscience and tone of America. In stressing the need for revival inside the church, Mr. Graham called for a "renewal of authoritative proclamation."

History tells us that Mr. Graham is right. Amos came to Bethel preaching. Jesus came to Nazareth preaching. Peter came to Jerusalem preaching. Paul went around the rim of the Mediterranean preaching. The reformers assaulted the entrenched wealth and power of Rome preaching. The early Americans came to these shores preaching. The pioneer preachers crossed the Alleghenies, the Cumberlands, and the Blue Ridge preaching. If the churches in America have a strength today at all, that strength is the consequence of faithful preaching.

The free pulpit is truth's last line of defense. Einstein, who has forever put the world in his debt with his genius, once confessed the birth of a new respect for the church. He observed that in the Germany of the middle and late twenties he foresaw the drift toward totalitarianism. At first, he looked to the statesmen of Germany to check Hitler's rise to power. Disappointed, he looked to the German military to resist Hitler's growing hold on the nation. But they, like Bismarck, capitulated to the Nazi leader. Then, Einstein said, he pinned his hope on the universities—the great free universities of Germany, some of the finest in the world—to block Hitler and his mad doctrine. But they also surrendered without a fight. Then Einstein confessed that the church, which had a pulpit dependent upon the state for its support and which he had completely overlooked, was the only segment of German society that dared to oppose Hitler openly. Einstein professed a new birth of respect for the church. Such men as Dietrich Bonhoeffer, Helmut Thielicke, Martin Niemoeller, and Otto Dibelius were men who stood in the tradition of Amos.

If the preacher of our day is to have any message at all, he and the congregation he serves must be willing to pay the price. There is a price to be paid in study, meditation, and prayer. Elton Trueblood, noted author and lecturer, spoke recently at North Carolina's Wake Forest College. He dealt with the fact that the congregation today wants its minister to be always available. Then he dropped a bombshell:

A minister who is always available is not worth enough when he is available. Christ left the multitudes when they needed him, but when he returned they needed him more. We all need to do what Christ did. He went aside to refresh and sustain himself. . . .

Hide some every day. Have time to pray, think and meditate. Let the wells fill up . . . you've got to be tough. If you don't watch out [about your time] you will become nothing more than a chore boy. Your task is to be a nourisher of people at deep places.[2]

Sometimes the expectations of the pew, as they look toward the pulpit, are not true to the heart of preaching as a function. Kermit Eby in "Soda Pop Religion" has said:

We have accepted the Coca-Cola concept of religion.
We produce an effervescent, scintillating, sparkling sermon,
Attractively bottled . . .
Pleasing to the customer, even if it causes a few
Spiritual hiccups, and available to all customers
At a fairly standard rate of the
Weekly contribution.
Every Sunday in the pulpit:
"The pause that refreshes."

Well, Amos came, not as a fresh and stimulating intellectual breeze, but as a fearsome tornado. When he had passed through Bethel, everything false had been stripped away.

That is the function of the preacher as he preaches.

The Focus of Preaching

When Amos stormed into Bethel, the eye of the storm was concentrated on the decadence of Israel. The people had been drifting on the spiritual seas of life, and when men drift, it is never toward God and spiritual things. The drift is always away.

We know that from personal experience. It is easier to cease to pray than to begin. It is simpler to drop out of church than to be faithful. It is more natural to be silent than to bear witness. It is harder to tithe than to spend money on ourselves. If we set the skiff of our lives adrift, the drift will be away from important things.

Israel had been adrift. Amos does not stutter as he reads his "bill of particulars":

> They sold the righteous for silver, and the poor for a pair of shoes; that pant after the dust of the earth on the head of the poor, and turn aside the way of the meek: and a man and his father will go in unto the same maid, to profane my holy name: And they lay themselves down upon clothes laid to pledge by every altar, and they drink the wine of the condemned in the house of their god (2:6-8).

To bring into focus the decadence of Israel, Amos sets before the imagination of his hearers a basket of summer fruit. The fruit has been plucked from the vine. It is lovely to behold, pleasing to smell. But already the fruit gnats are buzzing. Already the flesh of the fruit is unfirm. It is only a matter of time. Similarly, it is only a matter of logic that Israel—like a basket of summer fruit—will mold, rot, and be cast aside.

Were Amos to come to America, he would apply his parable to our lives, too. Some of us are trying to live on past spiritual momentum. Our Christian experience is all in the past tense. We have no good news that came just this morning.

We live in an age which is not kindly disposed toward spiritual things. All around us is the cacophony of sounds calling us to this pleasant diversion, that bright distraction. We have a secret suspicion that the little boy persuading his grandmother to go to the circus with him on prayer meeting night was right. Said the boy to his grandmother, "Why, Grandmother, if you would just go with me to the circus one time on Wednesday night, you would never want to go to prayer meeting again."

A lot of circuses are playing—not just on Wednesday night, but every night of the week. Some say that the movies, the novels, and the stage plays of any age bare its deepest maladies and its truest values. If that be true, then the arts of our day are raising fundamental questions about our manners and morals. Take the movies. The first movie really to shock the Western world was Italy's *La Dolce Vita,* which exposed the morally flabby life of Rome's high society. Next came *La Notte,* a study in twentieth-century boredom. Then came *The Silence,* a Swedish production, which prompted one United States lady critic to exclaim in print: "I couldn't believe my eyes!" "What she coudn't believe," writes *Life* magazine, "were scenes of lesbianism, voyeurism and incest." Then *Life* goes on to say, "But if you looked past these shock scenes, you recognized Bergman's preoccupation with what happens when people turn away from God and live only unto themselves."[3]

At this writing the latest film is a new release from England entitled *The Servant,* a pathetic story of a spoiled, selfish, snobbish young English gentleman who became a slave to alcoholism, sensualism, and masochism. The whole point of this latest film of international fame is that man in servility to himself is in the service of a poor master.

Amos' basket of summer fruit is a timely parable. We would do well to hear him out rather than to run him out. When he has done with us, we could do no better than to heed him. We may have to tear down some favorite shelter we have so painstakingly built. We may have to swallow pride, admit that our lives are a basket of summer fruit, and return to him who is the true vine. In Amos' day, Jeroboam II and his courtesan, Amaziah, led Israel in the rejection of Amos. But they had not rejected the preacher; they had rejected the God who sent him. Within a generation the jackals were howling in the deserted haunts of Bethel, the home of Amaziah, and in Samaria, the home of Jeroboam the king.

In the beginning we raised the question of the audacity of preaching: one man daring to speak for God. The record of

Amos is that God *did* speak through this uncomplicated son of the desert, that those who failed to hear and heed did so at their own ruin.

In our own day, we listen to a veritable babble of voices for seven days. These voices urge us to buy, to sell, to go, to stay. The Heavenly Father, who knows our inner beings, has given one more voice. It is the voice of his man—the preacher—saying, "Hear the word of the Lord."

Notes

1. Loudon Wainwright, "The Dying Girl That No One Helped," *Life*, LVI (April 10, 1964), 21.

2. J. Marse Grant, from an editorial in *Biblical Recorder*, no date available.

3. Thomas Thompson, "Movie Review: A New Twist on the Decadence Bit," *Life*, LVI (April 10, 1964), 12.

2

No Guarantee

Amos 5:18-19

Every generation has its dominant mood. The moods of twentieth-century America have varied from heroic self-sacrifice to irrepressible frivolity to economic and psychological depression to atomic war sobriety. The keynote of the sixties was sounded by the late President Kennedy in his inaugural address, when his brave words gave to the nation the challenge of courage in the face of imponderable dangers.

The generation in which Amos lived had its mood, too. It was a mood of pride, prosperity, and blind optimism. The catchword of Amos' era was "the day of the Lord." This phrase caught up all the idealistic dreams of fervid patriotism and a national character untested by the fires of war or adversity. The day of the Lord would bring judgment.

In one of the parables that Amos told he used this familiar watchword:

Woe unto you that desire the day of the Lord! to what end is it for you? the day of the Lord is darkness, and not light. As if a man did flee from a lion, and a bear met him; or went into the house, and leaned his hand on the wall, and a serpent bit him. Shall not the day of the Lord be darkness, and not light? even very dark, and no brightness in it? (5:18-20).

The brusque cadence, the staccato phrases, the graphic picture —Amos uses these to declare truths as timeless as the universe. This is not lavender and lace but blood and iron, as hard as the facts of life he deals with. Anyone who has lived any time at all senses that this preaching throbs with life; and in the pulsations, we can distinguish at least three truths which ring clear: inescapable judgment, hazardous life, and relentless time.

Inescapable Judgment

You will search in vain for the word "judgment" in Amos' parable. It is not there. But the thought is. It is found in the surprise ending of his story, which is about the day of the Lord. We anticipate the long sigh of relief once the door is slammed on the lion and the bear, but there is the cry of pain. The hunter (if that is what he was) does not escape; a worse fate befalls him. He dies ignominiously, not in valiant struggle with the lion or the bear, but from the poisoned prick of the viper.

If judgment is the underlying thought, the inevitability of judgment is the obvious truth. If we make the story run backward from conclusion to beginning like the motion picture projector sometimes does, we see that the hunter in the story is moving toward inevitable judgment even while making good his flight from the bear and his escape from the lion. Had he not been so exhausted from his ordeal, he might have been more careful.

The whole episode from beginning to end is one piece. The hunter was under judgment when he went out in the morning. He was under judgment when he matched his fleeting sprint to the lumbering pace of the bear. He was under judgment when he leaned against his own door. He was moving relentlessly, event by event, toward his own demise.

What is Amos saying here? Is it not that judgment both comes and is? We tend to think of judgment as some far-off event, which may be dreadful and unnerving, but it is not yet. We are like Christopher Morley's old Mandarin:

> In regard to Eternity (said the old Mandarin)
> I feel about it as I do about one of my teeth.
> Every now and then it gives me
> A devil of a twinge,
> And for a while
> I groan and can think of naught else.
> Then the anguish abates and I dismiss it from my mind.
> But I know, just the same,
> That some day
> I've got to go through with it.

We have ingenious ways of abating the anguish of such somber thoughts. Sometimes we manage to contrive a thorough-going distraction. We get on the merry-go-round that starts on Monday morning and doesn't run down until some time Saturday. By then we are so out of breath that all we can think of is a place to sit down and rest. If we go to church on Sunday, we are still numb from the last week's pace, and most of the lofty thoughts we are exposed to there sit on the top of our minds, never sinking in.

Like Morley's old Mandarin, some of us short-circuit the anguish of judgment by devoting all thought and might to the business of making a living, and if our living is assured, then to making a fortune.

Jesus told the story of one such man. When he is introduced to us, he is already gray at the temples. He is a self-made man, and he has made no significant mistakes. He is what the world would call "successful."

But Jesus sees a fatal flaw. There is a strange confusion in the man's mind. He thinks of all the symbols of his success—his barns, his fields, his grain—as extensions of himself. He is as tall as his barns are tall. He is as big as his fields are big. He is as full as his bins are full. Himself and his possessions are all of a piece. Somewhere along the way, he has lost his identity as a man!

Like the epitaph on a certain tombstone, "Born a man; died a grocer!" of him it might be said, "Born a man; died a landowner." He does not know it—this poor rich man—but the judgment of God was at work every day of those forty or fifty years, and now that he comes to the end of his days, he is exactly what he professes to be: a self-made man. He bears the image of his manufacturer. There has been nothing of God in his life.

Sometimes, inevitable judgment can be dismissed by the simple art of procrastination. "Tomorrow" is the fateful word. The devil, who is good with words, whispers "tomorrow, tomorrow, tomorrow" in our ears.

In George Bernard Shaw's play, *Back to Methusaleh,* there is a little by-play between Adam and Eve and the Serpent.

> Adam: Make me a beautiful word for doing a thing
>   tomorrow; for that surely is a great and
>   blessed invention.
> Serpent: Procrastination.
> Eve: That is a sweet word. I wish I had a serpent's
>   tongue.[1]

The devil is good with words, and one of his favorites is "tomorrow."

So Amos begins with the underlying thought that all our tomorrows taste of all our yesterdays, that judgment is but the sum of all our days.

Hazardous Life

We take a second look at Amos' parable, and we move from the inferred to the obvious. Amos is true to the heart of things in this parable. Life does not get easier as we go along; it gets harder. In the beginning of life's day, neither the lion nor the bear are a match for us. But as the sun sets—and here is the irony of life—even the small viper is too much.

Amos is thinking of the toll that time takes. As we get older, the stairs are steeper, the hills higher, the blocks longer, sleep more necessary. The *U.S. News & World Report* recently gave a statistical breakdown of the 189 million people in our population:

87 percent do not remember when there was no federal income tax.
71 percent were born since World War I.
64 percent do not remember the Prohibition era.
64 percent do not remember the start of the Roosevelt New Deal era.
56 percent were not born at the time of the 1929 stock market crash.
48 percent are too young to recall World War II.
22 percent have been born since the end of the Korean War.
 4 percent were not yet born when the first manned space shot was launched by the U.S.A.

But Amos is thinking of more than the toll of time; he is thinking of the risk and hazard involved in life. There is no guarantee against sudden death. We can buy all kinds of insurance to cushion the shock; we can buy none to eliminate it. It may be a grinding automobile crash, an ambulance ride in the dead of night, the ring of a long distance telephone call, the quiet conversation in the doctor's office, the auditor's report.

Recently, a typical, plain woman of a North Shore suburb in Sydney, Australia, wrote her pastor a letter about her own brush with the dark underside of life. Here is the letter.

Dear Sir:
I would like to tell you of my own experience. Some years ago I lost both my husband and only daughter (a beautiful girl of twenty-four) in the space of a few months. Both had long, linger-

ing illnesses and I was left a nervous wreck, thoroughly exhausted, too. I had two lads, one a young apprentice and the other a school boy. Neither was able to support himself.

As I sat in mental despair I realized that the boys, too, must have had terrific nervous strain. I decided to give them just what I was needing. . . . I set the meals a bit nicer, took extra care with the cooking, made their bedrooms more comfortable, and . . . generally built up the atmosphere of the home.

But, sir, I was the one that benefited. I proved to the full measure the text, "He that loseth his life shall find it." In losing my life to all their need, I saved my own. I came out of my sorrow quickly with balance and strength. I was able, after awhile, to take my place once more in the world. People thought I had got over it very quickly. No, sir, I never got over it, but the simple teaching of Jesus and the power of the Holy Spirit stood by me in desperate days and proved to me that there is a true remedy for all ills. After all, Jesus' injunction in dealing with the ills of mankind was: "Rise, take up your bed and walk," which was His way of saying, "Stand on your own two feet, shoulder your own responsibilities and get a move on."[2]

Amos' little story reminds us of the words of Longfellow in "A Psalm of Life":

> Life is real! Life is earnest!
> And the grave is not its goal;
> Dust thou art, to dust returnest,
> Was not spoken of the soul.[3]

Underlying Amos' parable is the thought of inescapable judgment. Explicit in the parable are the hazards bound up with life. Implicit in the parable is this final lesson: time, like the river, flows on. If you are ever going to make any change, change now!

Relentless Time

Thomas Wolfe, the gifted genius of Asheville, North Carolina, who came to an untimely end, titled one of his books *Of Time and the River.* That title suggests a thought congenial to the parable of Amos.

Imagine, if you will, somewhere along a meandering riverbank an old-fashioned gristmill. There is the mill race, the mill wheel, and the old mill house.

As we stand there before the old mill, we see two kinds of motion. The wheel goes around and around, steadily, slowly, imperturbably, moving in its fixed circle. That is one kind of motion. It is like the motion of the hands on our clocks, ever turning, ever moving.

But there is another kind of motion, the flow of the river. It is the flow of the river that makes the mill run. The water is diverted down the mill race; it tumbles over the wheel, but it moves relentlessly on toward the sea. It passes by the mill, and it is gone never to return. The same water may turn another mill in another place on another day, but never that same mill again.

That thought is faithful to Amos and faithful to life. While we pit our wits against the lions of life, while we match our cunning with the bears, time marches on. Now is the time to change. Were Amos to enlarge on his story, he would most likely say, "Now is the day; behold, now is the accepted time" (cf. 2 Cor. 6:2).

Some years ago when we lived in Louisville, Kentucky, a widow neighbor of ours lost her husband's mother. She had no children of her own, and the loss of this loved one opened afresh the wound of her husband's sudden passing a few years before. We attended the funeral in the St. Louis Cathedral of Louisville and tried to be helpful. One evening Mrs. Hillerick brought me this little poem and asked me to share it with others. "As you get older," she said, "you begin to realize just how true it is." I think it captures the implicit thought of Amos' parable of the bear, the lion, and the viper.

The clock of life is wound but once,
    And no man has the power
To tell just when the clock will stop
    At late or early hour.

Now is the only time you own—
    Live, love with a will;
Boast not of tomorrow, for
    The clock may then be still.

Notes

1. George Bernard Shaw, *Back to Methuselah* (London: Constable & Company, 1931), p. 12.
2. Source unknown.

3

Amazing Grace

Micah 7:16-20

Micah came from the country. A rustic man of the soil, he was a sentimentalist whose loyalties never swerved from the country man and country man's concerns. His home was in Gilead. A few miles to the north was Jerusalem, where the great Isaiah was prophet. The geographical distance from Gilead to Jerusalem was but a few miles; the social and economic distance was the distance between two worlds. In Jerusalem lived the absentee landlord, the banker, and the nobility. But Micah's sympathies were not there. He would have agreed whole-heartedly with Bobby Burns, who said:

> Princes and lords are but the breath of kings,
> "An honest man's the noblest work of God."
> > "The Cotter's Saturday Night"

Micah had his doubts about honest men who might live in Jerusalem.

Essentially, Micah was a poet. His approach to life was an emotional one. His words were always heavy with feeling. From the beginning of his career, Micah used strong words because he was moved by strong feelings. In his style we see the man.

Scholars tell us that Micah's writings may be divided into two parts, having come from different periods in his lifetime. The first five chapters come from Micah's earlier years, and they are afire with the burning social issues of the day. As we read them we can feel natural indignation at the economic and social injustice which his neighbors and friends were suffering. For Micah, who lived on the land, the land question was the great question, and that question stirred strong feelings. Micah was outraged at the injustice of absentee landlords, living idly in Jerusalem, taking nearly half the farmer's toil in rent.

Part two of Micah, which begins with chapter 6 and goes to the end of the book, while reflecting a mellower spirit, still breathes with the passion of a man who feels deeply. In this latter portion, Micah feels more sadness than outrage. The occasion of his sadness is that men are so blind to their own inner needs, so impervious to the needs of others, so resistant to the grace of God. He cannot understand it. The last sentences of his book, uttered in broken sobs, are an expression of wonder at the amazing grace of God:

Who is a God like unto thee, that pardoneth iniquity, and passeth by the transgression of the remnant of his heritage? he retaineth not his anger for ever, because he delighteth in mercy. He will turn again, he will have compassion upon us; he will subdue our iniquities; and thou wilt cast all their sins into the depths of the sea (7:18-19).

From youth to age Micah is the "feeling" man, the poet, who speaks from his heart. Yet, underlying his feelings—outrage in youth and sadness in age—are certain presuppositions. Without these presuppositions, Micah's feelings might have run wild. With them his feelings run true to the very heart of life itself.

What are these presuppositions?

First, that there *is* a right and a wrong.

Second, that to do wrong is to be a wrongdoer, and to have to bear the consequent burden of guilt.

Third, that God will subdue our iniquities and cover our sins with his grace.

Right and Wrong

Juliet Lowell wrote a book a few months back entitled *Dear VIP*. It was a series of letters written to prominent people about random subjects. One of the letters, addressed to the late President Kennedy, went like this:

President of the United States
The White House
Washington, D. C.

Dear President Kennedy:
    My name is John too and I'm President of my class. Please write and tell me what things a good President shouldn't be caught doing.

                              (Signed) John S.

We smile at such innocence. Yet, many of us unconsciously have a definition of right and wrong that is relative, relative to a lot of things: our feelings, our construction of circumstances, extenuating stresses, and on and on.

As I was thinking about this idea, I remembered taking my car into the garage to have a little work done on the electrical system. It was under guarantee, and when the bill came it was for nearly six dollars. In the meantime, I discovered that the mechanic had left a pair of electrician's pliers in the trunk of my car. Until I got that bill, I had intended to take those pliers back at the first opportunity. But after the bill, almost unconsciously, I somehow never found the opportunity. When I stopped to look at the situation honestly, I knew immediately what had happened. I had decided that in this particular situation I had been overcharged, that I could rectify the situation by just keeping the pliers for a while—maybe for good—if I could successfully forget where they had come from. In a case like that, right and wrong were relative. Here was something I could do without getting caught.

Haven't we all done things like that? The embezzler never intends to be a thief; he only intends to borrow. The pressed church member never intends to use his tithe to pay bills; he only wishes to pay the most pressing creditor. The adulterer never intends to break up his marriage; he only intends to do the friendliest possible thing.

Historically, there are two views of right and wrong. One is the view I have been expounding: that all right and wrong is relative to something else. But there is another view. The Bible teaches that all right and wrong is absolute; it is not relative to anything. There is a right; there is a wrong; if we are sincere, we can find which is which.

We all betray ourselves in this matter, because we usually have very little trouble identifying the wrong someone else does. It is only when we do wrong ourselves that it is not quite so definite.

Admittedly, judgments in the area of right and wrong can become quite complex, particularly when we think of social justice. Even when we recognize the right, we may be impeded by other valid considerations. But in our own lives, and in our own affairs, we can usually define right and wrong with a minimum of error—if we want to. The truth is that all too often we do not want to. We act; then we arrange our reasons. Reason is a faithful servant; it will support any position, any decision, any choice we wish to make.

Micah—this feeling man—knows how feelings of want and need can betray us. But also, he knows that underlying life is an absolute ethic, a God-given ethic—a definite right and a definite wrong.

Wrongdoers and the Burden of Wrongdoing

The second presupposition in Micah's view of life is quite simple. It follows from the first, namely, that calling wrong right does not make it right. Wrong and right do not change places so blithely. I can pursue a wrong course, even persuade myself that it is all right for me, but that does not make it right. It is still wrong, and in doing the wrong I became a wrongdoer.

This is where conscience comes in. When I become a wrongdoer, or contemplate such, the voice of the "warner" is heard deep inside me. The dialogue between the wrongdoer and his conscience is quite interesting, never dull. Do you remember those sequences in *Priscilla's Pop* where Priscilla's conscience is pictured as a small Priscilla with wings and halo, hovering about, haranguing Priscilla about a course of action which she is considering? What makes that a proper subject for the funny paper? That it *is* funny! The rationalization of Priscilla and her conscience is so transparently outlandish as to be funny.

It would be funny in real life if it weren't so tragic.

Dr. Pierce Harris, pastor of the First Methodist Church, Atlanta, Georgia, writes a daily column for the *Atlanta Constitution*. In one of his recent columns Dr. Harris said:

I've got a few members who skip off every once in a while and go fishing on Sunday. When I miss them from the congregation, I don't sleep well that night and I am afraid to pick up the paper Monday morning for fear that I will see where the boat turned over and they drowned during that golden Sabbath Day while enjoying "God's great outdoors."

So far, I've been spared that pain of trying to think up something halfway truthful to say at such a sad eventuality. I hope I never have to face it.

Back some years ago I was asked to go over 500 miles to conduct the funeral of a friend. How I ever came by such a friend is beyond me. He never darkened the door of a church. His language would make a sailor blush. He played golf every Sunday except when the mackerel were running, and then he was on the high seas busy with his deep sea rod and reel. With the funeral on the Sabbath I could not get away but I made some helpful suggestions about the burial service:

Have the golf pro read a few lines from the rule book, let some close friend recall some exciting shots he made during his lifetime, call the "captain" of his fishing boat into the picture long enough to tell how "devoted" he was to his first love . . . fishing . . . then drag his casket aboard, take it out beyond the jetties . . . and dump it overboard.

That seemed appropriate to me . . . *finished up like he lived.* It didn't please some other people though! I got a lot of letters, among them one that said, "You don't deserve to be a preacher." But, talking about what people deserve, would you say the man deserved a Christian burial when all his life he ignored God and neglected his own soul?[1]

Sooner or later, the wrongdoer gets caught up in the tissue of rationalizations, half-truths, and fictions by which he has called his wrong right, and he stands naked and ashamed of what he is. That is what Genesis tells us; that is what life tells us; that is what the Bible warns us.

Grace for Guilt

There is another way to handle our wrongdoing besides trying to cover up; that is to own up.

What saddened Micah was that his own fellow countrymen would not own up to their sins. Theirs was a foolish rebellion which refused to face its guilt.

That is what saddens a preacher, too. There are only these two alternatives—cover up or own up. If we cover up, refuse the gift of God's grace, then the preacher knows that sooner or later the storm of God's wrath will fall. There is really no other way.

"All have sinned, and come short of the glory of God." That is

God's verdict. We are wrongdoers. But such a statement is no gospel; it only prepares us for the gospel. The gospel is this: "While we were yet sinners, Christ died for us" (Rom. 5:8).

Micah, on the far side of Calvary, marveled at the forgiving grace of our God. But how little Micah knew of the whole joyous picture!

For those of us on this side of Calvary who know what it cost God to forgive in Jesus, we can only say with John Newton:

> Amazing grace! how sweet the sound,
> That saved a wretch like me!
> I once was lost, but now am found,
> Was blind, but now I see.
>
> 'Twas grace that taught my heart to fear,
> And grace my fears relieved;
> How precious did that grace appear
> The hour I first believed!
>
> Thro' many dangers, toils and snares,
> I have already come;
> 'Tis grace hath bro't me safe thus far,
> And grace will lead me home.

Notes

1. Pierce Harris, quoted in *First Baptist Beacon,* May 21, 1964, p. 2.

4

Valley of Achor

Hosea 2:14-17

The ecstasy and the anguish of Hosea's domestic life reflected the transparent truth of God's ecstasy and anguish over Israel. Sixteen times in his fourteen chapters Hosea uses the hateful word "whoredom" to describe the sin of Israel. Hosea did not *tell* a parable; his life *was* a parable of the grieving, constant, unrequited love of God.

The tragedy of Hosea's hearth taught him the tragedy of Ephraim's altar. The esoteric fertility cults of Baal and Ashtoreth were Israel's undoing, even as the mysterious and sensual rites of Baal worship had been Gomer's undoing. The driving necessity which impelled Hosea to reclaim Gomer his wife, even to buying her back out of slavery, also impelled God to reclaim his people. Hosea knew God could not let Ephraim go; that if the final break came, it would come from Ephraim. But Hosea would not believe Ephraim had sunk so low as to finally break with her God. Instead, Hosea hoped for reconciliation and a restructuring of the relationship on surer and more constant grounds.

One of the symbols Hosea used to express this lovely hope was taken from a popular tradition out of the wilderness wanderings, his people's history for seven hundred years. That symbol was the Valley of Achor.

We find the grim story of Achor in Joshua 2. You may recall its essential features. Moses was dead; Joshua was the new leader. Under his command the Israelites had triumphantly crossed the Jordan. By cunning and wit reinforced with a vibrant faith, the formidable walls of Jericho, which sat at the head of the Valley of Achor, had tumbled down. The whole land seemed to lie defenseless before them.

The next important military objective was the village of Ai, up the valley a few miles. A reconnaissance party came back advising that Ai was not worth an all-out effort; a party of three thousand warriors would overwhelm it.

But it was not Ai that was overwhelmed; it was the three thousand. Israel suffered a smarting defeat at Ai. The heady spirit after Jericho became the heavy heart after Ai. Even Joshua asked the dark question: "Wherefore hast thou at all brought this people over Jordan, to deliver us into the hand of the Amorites, to destroy us?" (Josh. 7:7). It was a black and somber moment there in the Valley of Achor.

It is always darkest just before the dawn. When Joshua had composed himself, it was discovered that the cause of the defeat at Ai was not the valor of the enemy, but the sin in the camp of Israel. Achan, one of Joshua's soldiers, had taken from Jericho what is simply called "the accursed thing." That was the reason for the defeat.

The story concludes when Achan is found out—just as our sin always finds us out. The sin is judged in the Valley of Achor, and Achor, which had been such a devastatingly difficult defeat, became the door of hope for Joshua and all Israel.

That, in brief, is the story of Achor. Now, these seven hundred years later, Hosea uses that familiar bit of national history to say to his beloved Ephraim: "Your Valley of Achor may become a door of hope."

What is it Hosea pleads for with this "Valley of Achor"

symbol? A path beginning in despair and concluding in hope. The despair is the present spiritual and national decay; the hope is a vision of the purified and transformed people that may emerge out of this present darkness.

Hosea makes the journey from despair to hope in four stages. The first milestone is a *reminder,* namely: familiarity often breeds contempt at worst, indifference at best. The second milestone is an *assertion:* by God's grace, nothing is lost, not even our wrong steps. The third is a *definition:* Achor becomes hope only when we face our failure. The last milestone is a *reassurance:* God's love is big enough to cover our false starts.

Familiarity Breeds Contempt

Ephraim was in his spiritual maturity. Long ago as a child, he had leaned heavily upon his God. But that was long ago; Ephraim had grown older and (as he thought) wiser. As Ephraim had grown fat and gray he had lost his sense of dependency. For long years God was a part of the furniture of his mind, but only one piece. Alongside God were other pieces. Some had grown more attractive, more predominant in his mind than this old *antique* piece called God, handed down from generation to generation through seven hundred years. As a matter of fact, God had been shoved back in a corner. God was not the most important thing to Ephraim, not nearly.

Hosea peered through the veil of history to see that Ephraim, like Achan of old, had become attached to "the accursed thing." Here was history repeating itself, but on a far larger scale. In Achor it was one man; now it was a nation.

Could it be that we too need Hosea's reminder of the deadly peril of the proximate? Can the reality of faith lose its hold on us?

All of life tells us that this is not only possible, but quite probable. The only remedy is to recognize that routine is our deadly enemy. Routine and his twin, humdrum, stalk every marriage and every experience of faith. When we sink into a comfortable routine, "the first, fine careless rapture" expires for want of air. Routine is the bugaboo of middle life and middle age; routine and familiarity are the deadly foes of a vital faith.

One of the memorable scenes in an English novel of some years ago describes how a little boy named Bron goes to church for the first time with his governess. He watches with interest every part of the service and when the preacher stands in the pulpit Bron hears him give out a piece of terrible news. It is about a brave and kind man who was nailed to a cross . . . ferociously hurt a long time ago . . . who feels a dreadful pain even now, because there was something not done that he wants them to do. Little Bron thinks that the preacher is telling the story because a lot of people are there and they will do something about it. Bron is impatient, on the edge of his pew. He can scarcely wait to see what the first move will be to right this terrible injustice. But nothing happens. He sits quietly and decides that after the service someone will do something about it. Little Bron weeps, but nobody else seems upset. The service is over, the people walk away as if they had not heard such terrible news, as if nothing remarkable had happened. As Bron leaves the church, he is trembling. His governess looks at him and says, "Bron, don't take it to heart—someone will think you are queer."

It is with such an attitude that Hosea begins. To be careless about spiritual things is the first storm warning. Do not be presumptuous in your relationship with God. It can only bring on heartbreak and pain.

Nothing Is Lost

But Hosea addresses himself to a people who have already presumed. The edge has been off in their relationship to God for generations. They have already sown to the wind; the deadly spiral of the whirlwind looms on the horizon. What now?

It is here that Hosea rises to a loftier stature. Hosea understands that out of failure and sin we can wrest some good. Not even our wrong steps are a total loss. We can learn from them.

Pain is part of the learning process. It is sometimes unpleasant to work, but it is more unpleasant to take the consequences of not working. The schoolboy may not like to get his lessons, but he likes even less to take a failing grade from the teacher.

But more than that is involved. Hosea is affirming that God has a special regard and a special treatment for good intentions that go awry, for holy dreams defiled, for lives that somehow have gotten all messed up.

Just because we are in Achor does not mean that we are through. God knows what the pain of stifled things can be.

> God has a special place for still-born things,
> The things that never were and should have been:
> The little songs no singer ever sings,
> The beauty of a picture hung unseen,
> A noble heart that loved with no return,
> And deeds well meant which somehow turned out ill,
> A lovely flame that vainly tried to burn
> But could not last, though all the winds were still,
> The early flower that no one ever sees
> Making its way through ground iced hard with sleet,
> A Caesar to whom no man bends his knees,
> The Christ-like smile that meets each fresh defeat:
> God treats them very tenderly for He
> Knows what the pain of stifled things can be.[1]

Not even our sin need be a total waste.

Facing Our Failure

Achor lies very close to the surface of the third step of Hosea's journey from despair to hope. Achor meant only defeat until Israel faced the sin of Achan, dealt with it, and started fresh.

It is the same with most of our falterings. Perhaps we have not really defined our problem; or if defined, we have not honestly dealt with it, faced it, started out fresh. Too many of us spend our energies in running down friends, sidestepping our responsibilities, pushing our luck. Hosea calls for a more responsible approach to life.

Most of us are content to drift along until things get so intolerable that they prod us toward definition of the problem and reflection on ways of solving it. Sometimes it takes sleepless nights and wet pillows before we get life arranged the way it works best. An unknown poet has said it beautifully:

Things come plain in the middle of the night.
Roiled water clears; we see what's at bottom,
The rock silted over, the waterlogged tree.
This turns to that before us—ask not how it happens
We come back fledged with power from the great gulf entered.

Old puzzlements resolve themselves as if by some enchantment.
We swim up out of sleep like the diver with his pearl.
As fearless as a drawing made by the sure hand of a child,
Life assumes an outline; we have a hint to go by.[2]

And nearly every time, when we get to the bottom of the problem, we find that it involves our relationship with God. If the center of life is not right, the rest cannot be. When the foundation is not sure, the house will not stand.

One greater than Hosea put the thought of Hosea quite concisely: "Seek ye first the kingdom of God, . . . and all these things will be added unto you."

God's Love Covers Our Sin

So we have come thus far with Hosea, even to the door of hope. But it is only a door. How do we enter in? By believing simply this: God's love is big enough to cover our false starts and our broken dreams, and give us ground on which to stoop and begin building again.

Israel was stronger for having Achor to remember. Many a marriage is stronger for having a certain painful episode in its history. Many a Christian is stronger for having a memory of some private hell.

Hosea has a word for those who are depressed and confused: Achor can be a door of hope. To those who repent and who honestly seek to build again with God, there can be an entering through that door of hope into God's meadowlands of fulfilment and joy. You say, I wish I could be sure of that; do you have any evidence?

Open your New Testament. The first Gospel was written by Matthew. Matthew's life was limp, empty, and futile when Jesus challenged him to become a disciple. But all that was changed when he passed through the door of hope.

Next is Mark. Mark had messed up things in his life so badly that the apostle Paul wanted to have nothing more to do with him. The only serious difference Paul ever had with his dear friend Barnabas was over John Mark. But John Mark learned by his wrong attitude and was at Paul's side when he died. He served with Peter at Rome in Paul's place. That is how we came to have his Gospel.

Luke is the next. He was a physician in Troas when Paul went to him as a patient. Apparently Luke's life was out of kilter. Christ became his door of hope. He gave us both a Gospel and the book of Acts.

John was known for his violent temper when he met Jesus. His nickname was "son of thunder." But Jesus opened to him the door of hope, and in later years he was known as the "apostle of love."

Turn to the book of Romans. There are at least twelve more

books in your New Testament written by this same man. His name is Paul. Before Christ opened hope's door to him, this man was in the grim, silent despair of a life based on violence, ambition, self-serving. But he passed through that door of hope and out of his vale of Achor. In the service of Christ he found meaning and purpose, and his life fell into a pattern of wondrous beauty.

You who are in Achor! You stand at the door of hope today.

Notes

1. Dorothy Quick, "A Special Place," *The Questing Mind*, eds. Halford E. Luccock and Frances Brentano (New York: Coward-McCann, Inc., 1947), p. 317.

2. Quoted by Theodore P. Ferris, Rector of Trinity Church, Boston, in a privately published manuscript, March 22, 1964.

5

A Silly Dove

Hosea 7:9-11

The Indian Summer had not long to last. Already the haze was on the horizon and the nights crisp with a touch of winter. The season was far spent. Hosea lived in the last days of the little nation of Israel, which he fondly called Ephraim. The signs of the time were read clearest in the sudden starts and shifts in the country's foreign policy. Caught between two great powers, Assyria to the north and Egypt to the south, the uneasy and expendable kings of Israel played a dangerous and deadly game of international power politics. It was the age-old tactic of "playing both ends against the middle"; but in this instance, Israel was caught in the middle and crushed.

Within ten years following the death of the strong king Jeroboam II, who died in 746 B.C., the little nation had had five kings. Man-made and man-murdered, they came and they went with violence and force. With each change of national leadership there was a corresponding shift in the national course. The monarchy was a weather vane, turning willy-nilly with the vagrant winds that were blowing Israel ever closer to the shoals. The instability of the throne was a faithful reflection of the instability of the nation—a nation without conviction, without moral strength, without faith.

In such a desperate time, Hosea could not be silent. The very hopelessness of the times prompts him to deliver one of his most penetrating analyses. With pounding in his breast and a catch in his throat, Hosea diagnoses the ills of Ephraim. In a rapid thrust Hosea catches and holds the mortal maladies of his beloved nation:

"Ephraim is a cake not turned. Strangers have devoured his strength, and he knoweth it not: yea, gray hairs are here and there upon him, yet he knoweth not. . . . Ephraim also is like a silly dove without heart . . . (7:8-9, 11).

You recognize the metaphors: the half-baked scone; the unrecognized, but advancing years; the silly dove. In these figures Hosea was saying something timeless. It was about his own time, to be sure, but it is about our time, too.

Life Out of Balance

Some scholars believe that Hosea at one time in his life was a baker. Here is one of the pictures cut from life that makes them think so. The reference is to a flat, round cake which is baked on hot stones. This particular scone was never turned; it was half-baked.

Half-baked—that is the heart of this first malady. The half-baked scone suggests a lack of balance, a weakness in national character, a lack of proportion and perspective in Ephraim's approach to life.

Of course, Hosea had specific circumstances in mind, and he did not hesitate to amplify his truth. But what is his truth for us?

Is it not that we must maintain some sense of balance in our lives, some degree of proportion? If this is what Hosea is saying to us, perhaps we had better examine the patient to see if the diagnosis fits.

Let the patient be our times. One of the vital appendages of our time is the rising business of communication. *Rapid* is the only word which can describe this burgeoning field since that December 12, 1901, when Marconi transmitted his first transoceanic telegraph message. You will remember that the message was a question: "What hath God wrought?"

More recently, America successfully launched Telstar, enabling us to send not mere dots and dashes, but the image and the voice across a wide expanse of land and ocean. It is interesting to examine the first programs transmitted from our modern Telstar. America used her portion of the time to transmit an inning of a baseball game. France used her portion of this international program to take us to a Paris night club. Only Britain, seeming to sense the meaning of this event, used the time for a discussion of a serious nature.

While we have improved vastly the means of communication, the content seems to have lost its meaning.

The American is "the man on the go." To take time for meditation is a kind of national aversion; to loaf is a kind of venial sin. We must be on the move. Speed seems to be one of our goddesses. Some wag has said:

> Since we travel by jet,
> The impression I get
> Is that things are decidedly humming.
> Since we're faster than sound—
> When we get on the ground—
> If we listen, we can hear ourselves coming.

America does not live in the same house or the same city for any great length of time; not any more. The United Press reported recently that according to Atlas Van Lines, Incorporated, forty-one million persons can be expected to change address, local and long distance, this year.

Paul Elmen writes in his book *The Restoration of Meaning to Contemporary Society* a word of warning to the modern American minister. He offers the judgment that modern man is bored to tears, and when he comes to the church of Jesus Christ with his boredom and his loneliness, all we offer to do is reshuffle his activities. Perhaps that needs to be done, but that is not enough.

Robert McAfee Brown sounds almost the same note in his book *The Significance of the Church* when he writes that the man who is inactive in the church may have learned this response. The modern American says quite honestly: "I joined the church in the last town in which we lived. The first thing they did was put me on the bowling team and my wife in the kitchen. Now I am going to settle down and be a comfortable pagan."

Hosea would make a plea for a genuine sense of proportion and balance. He would not condemn activity; he would advise only that rest be observed as well. He would not smash our modern communication devices; he would counsel that they be used genuinely to enrich life. He would not condemn our times of fellowship around the table; he would urge us to saturate our conversation with godliness.

I leave for you the question of balance in your own life. A study made by the *Harvard Business Review* indicated that the average executive spent 42.7 hours at his office or place of business; 21 hours in sports, hobbies, TV, movies, visiting friends, relaxing; 9.4 hours at home with the family; 2.7 hours at the church. This may indicate an imbalance not only of time, but of values. It is not that we need to spend more time in church, though some of us certainly need that; it is that we need to strike a better balance all the way through our lives.

Unrecognized Condition

The second metaphor is an all-too-familiar page from life,

especially for those who are in middle age or past. In a voice that mixes scorn with a sob, Hosea says that his people are streaked with gray hairs, and they *know it not.* The pathos is not in the gray hair; it is in the lack of recognition of a condition. Could this be true of us?

If art and literature are the truest reporters of the character of any age, then we may shudder at what the modern impressionistic school of art is saying about us. Lewis Mumford confirms my own suspicion about what the modern cubistic, depersonalized art is saying, in this estimate:

In those special realms of art, above all painting, that once recorded the greatest freedom and creativeness, we find in our age that the symbols of the deepest expression of emotion and feeling are a succession of dehumanized nightmares. . . . The maimed fantasies, the organized frustrations that we see in every comprehensive exhibition of painting today are the evidence of a deeper personal abdication. . . . Man has become an exile in this mechanical world. . . . When society is healthy, the artist re-inforces its health; but when it is ailing, he too easily re-inforces its ailments.[1]

And someone else has commented on our age: "One of the paradoxes of our time is that while few ages have borne more tragic evidence of sin, few ages have been less conscious of it."[2]

What does this say to us who are Christians? I believe it says that we must come to terms with the fact that being a Christian means belonging to the minority; it means living a life that is distinctively different; it means seeking to pack content into every day and every chance meeting. The New Testament Christians understood this, and one wrote to the others:

For the time is come that judgment must begin at the house of God: and if it first begin at us, what shall the end be of them that obey not the gospel of God? And if the righteous scarcely be saved, where shall the ungodly and the sinner appear? Wherefore let them that suffer according to the will of God commit the keeping of their souls to him in well doing, as unto a faithful Creator (1 Pet. 4:17-19).

Unreasoning Folly

This third and final metaphor does not mean as much to most of us as it did to Hosea's hearers. The fowler is not a part of our life; his devices are not well known.

A favorite bird of the fowler was the dove. She was easy to confuse, and therefore, easy to snare. "There is nothing more simple than the dove," says an Arabic proverb. Simple and unsuspicious, the dove would fly thoughtlessly from the danger of the pursuing hawk into the snare of the fowler. The dove was well known for its shortsightedness.

Hosea likens his Ephraim to the silly dove, "without understanding." Of course, there are overtones of a dated and local foreign policy in that figure of speech; there are also implications of a timeless and universal moral. Men, like Ephraim and the silly dove, fall into the snare because they fail to take the long look. They, like the silly dove, are without understanding.

"Without understanding"; what does the Bible mean by such an allegation? What kind of person is it who is "without understanding"?

Briefly, it is a person who has not yet seen to the heart of things. He may accrue wisdom, but without understanding. In fact, the Bible warns about wisdom without understanding: "Wisdom is the principal thing; therefore get wisdom: and with all thy getting, get understanding" (Prov. 4:7).

When one has thrust down to the heart of things, he understands that under, in, and over this world is a loving Father, who has been revealed in the person of Jesus. For those of us who are on this side of Bethlehem and the New Testament, true wisdom is to find Christ in every moment, every relationship, and every new understanding. One poet has put it this way:

I see His blood upon the rose,
And in the stars the glory of His eyes;
His body gleams amid eternal snows,
His tears fall from the skies.

All pathways by His feet are worn,
His strong heart stirs the very beating sea;
Rocks are His written words—
His cross is every tree.[3]

A man who has a vision of life like that is not likely to be a silly dove, without understanding. God, as revealed in Christ, is at the center of life, and with him all life has meaning.

But ah! pity the man who has not made such a discovery. He, indeed, is a silly dove without understanding.

Do you know the story of Aaron Burr? His father, the Reverend Aaron Burr, was the second president of Princeton University, at that time the College of New Jersey. His mother was the daughter of the famous New England preacher, Jonathan Edwards. His parents died while he was quite young, but they had bequeathed to him an unusual legacy of personality and intelligence. While a student at Princeton, the younger Burr came under mighty conviction. He went to see the college president, who advised him to wait until the excitement had died down. The advice was fatal. Burr waited. Torn by his irritating indecision, he called to Christ: "If you let me alone, I'll let you alone." He never seriously considered becoming a Christian again.

Burr went on to a brilliant military career in the Revolutionary Army. After independence, he married the widow of a British officer, Theodosia Prevost. Success followed success until he came within one vote of being president of the United States, a decision finally rendered by the House of Representatives in favor of Thomas Jefferson.

Now this brilliant man was stymied. In frustration, he challenged Alexander Hamilton to a duel and slew him. Later in a western land grab scheme, he was charged with treason by President Jefferson. Though exonerated, Burr left the United States for Europe. There, his morals sank. He died some years later in disgrace. The citizens of his hometown would not allow a tombstone to mark his grave. Today, the name of Aaron Burr is associated with infamy in American history.

That in its most dramatic form is what Hosea would warn us against: a life without moorings, a life without the Father whom we know in Christ. To fail to have him is to be a "silly dove" and guilty of unreasoning folly.

Notes

1. Lewis Mumford, quoted in "The Image of God and the Landscape of Death," *Christianity Today*, VIII (May 8, 1964), 34.

2. Exposition by Harold Cooke Phillips, "Hosea," *The Interpreter's Bible*, ed. Nolan B. Harmon (12 vols.; New York: Abingdon-Cokesbury Press, 1951), VI, 638.

3. Joseph Mary Plunkett, "I See His Blood," *Masterpieces of Religious Verse*, ed. James Dalton Morrison (New York: Harper & Brothers, 1948), p. 201.

6

Court Day

Isaiah 1:1-20

Some men are endowed with gifts of body and spirit that seem to mark them for greatness. Such was the man Isaiah. Since the fourth century before Christ, there has been a persistent tradition that he was of the royal family. Whether he had royal blood or not, we may never be sure. This much we know: he walked through life with a regal bearing. He gave to all his public utterances a style, a scope, and a cadence that time has not eroded. He is still the peer of Israel's prophets.

A man is never understood apart from the times that make him. Isaiah's times were chaotic. The old Davidic kingdom—or what was left of it—was disintegrating. The northern sector which had gone its independent way more than two hundred years before was going under for the last time. The fate of this northern brother was a bad omen for Judah. The future was dark, the prospects foreboding.

It was about this time that Hezekiah ascended the throne of Judah, a mere shadow of her former greatness. But on this monarch and in this little nation resided all the hopes of Israel and, indeed, of the whole world. It may have been the sheer desperation of the times, but this coronation seems to have triggered Isaiah, spurring him into a period of greatness unmatched in

40

prophetic Israel and indeed, in few periods of religious history.

We turn first to chapter one. Chronologically, this is not the first of Isaiah's public declamations. It has a style and a structure that belies the novice. This is the work of the master. It comes first because it is choicest among the prophetic creations of the man.

We are introduced to a cosmic court. In this grand assize, the Ruler of all the earth is both plaintiff and judge. Called to witness is heaven and earth. In the docket is pathetic, trembling, pitiable little Judah. She is confused by the swirling events that have swept away her independence, that have challenged her patriotism, that have mocked her faith. She appears dazed, scarcely aware of what is going on. It is too much for her to take in. She is lost on the sea of nemesis.

This is the genius of Isaiah at work, dramatically portraying the pain and the pathos of the bad conscience and the guilty heart. His speech is addressed, of course, to his own countrymen. The citations are contemporary. But it speaks a timeless language, and the dynamics of guilt and forgiveness are eternal. Entering Isaiah's courtroom, as we shall, we find that it speaks to us even as it must have spoken to Judah.

In that courtroom the case against Judah moves swiftly through three steps. The first is the *argument* of the plaintiff, who, we must remember, is the Lord of all the earth. Then comes the *charge*. Finally, there is *the offer of settlement*. I believe we might capture this movement of thought with three words: revelation, resistance, and reconcilation.

Revelation

Isaiah is personalizing heaven and earth and calling them into court as witness against pitiable little Judah. Does this seem odd to you? What is it Isaiah is getting at?

In beautiful simplicity Isaiah has expressed one of the most profound thoughts of all human insight. In a single sentence Isaiah is saying that the *God who is high is also the God who is near.*

One of the fundamental mysteries of life is that the Heavenly Father has so little to say, that God is silent so much of the time. The common human experience is that when we need God most he seems to be farthest away. When the contrary winds of life are blowing and our prayers have leaden wings, the silence of God can seem almost oppressive.

This is the God who is high, away, out of reach.

But Isaiah says that in actual fact God is quite near. The prophet calls upon heaven and earth to witness.

We see this nearness in the Bible's description of the creation. The Bible presents the shimmering, dew-fresh creation as the substance of God's spoken word. Nine times in Genesis 1 the Bible says, "And God said. . . ." Each order of the creation is introduced with the majestic words, "And God said. . . ." The Bible is telling us that God *is* speaking through the created orders of the world and of space as we know them. Every star, every planet, every hill and dale, all the animals of the forest and barnyard, the fish in the lakes and the rivers and the seas, the birds on the wing, the flowers in the field, the changing seasons—all these and many more are echoes of the voice of God.

So God begins his case by establishing that he is not removed from us. He whispers to us from the treetops, and he caresses us with the morning breeze.

All things bright and beautiful, All things great and small,
All things wise and wonderful; Our Father made them all.
Each little flower that opens, Each little bird that sings;
He made their glowing colors, He made their tiny wings.

Cold wind in the winter, Pleasant summer sun,
Ripe fruits in the garden; He made them ev'ry one.

He gave us eyes to see them, And lips that we might tell
How good is God our Father Who doeth all things well.[1]

Thus the heavens and earth can be called to witness against
Judah. God who is high is also near. He speaks in our known
and familiar world.

But God speaks in a voice even more familiar than that.
Corresponding to the witness of the external world is the witness
of an internal world as well. God has given the "starry expanse
above"; he has also given the "moral law within." Usually, we
call it conscience. As Isaiah said: "The ox knoweth his owner,
and the ass his master's crib: but Israel does not know, my people
do not *reflect*" (v. 3).

It is an insult to presume that God is either a fool or stupid.
God is not happy with the person who goes blithely through life
assuming that "Somebody up there likes me." God does more than
that; he loves us. Love is not foolishly indulgent; it is intelligently
demanding. The voice of the conscience is God's voice, making
his moral demands upon us. These are the lines within which we
may find happiness, joy, and fulfilment. "Stay within these lines,"
says this warning voice, "and all life pulls with you. Get out of
these lines, and all of life pulls against you. And it will pull you
down."

This is revelation. It is not something mysterious, not magical.
Isaiah puts religion on a rational basis. It is a "reasonable inter-
course between one intelligent Being and another."[2] God is no
fool, and he is not stupid. To assume as much is to assume too
much.

Resistance

The uniform history of man, and of our own lives, is that we
do not want to heed this inner voice. We imagine we can find
genuine fulfilment outside the invisible lines this voice draws. So

the voice continues to speak. We are compelled to listen to things which we do not wish to hear. The voice returns again and again, like the sea returns to the shore. God upheaves the soul as well as the ocean. Every man, along with Judah, has his days in God's court.

And yet, we seek ways of refuge. We search out devices to quiet the disturbing voice, to check the disquieting thought.

Sometimes we take refuge in the *functions* of religion. Judah was exceedingly religious. The people multiplied their altars and oblations, but it was only perfunctory.

That thought makes us sit up straight. How many of us are just going through motions? Is that what we do when we worship? Does our worship make any genuine difference in the kinds of persons we are after the hour is over?

It is interesting that sometimes those with the most Christ-like and charitable spirits are those who hold the church off at arm's length. Christians can hide in church and sometimes do. God's children sometimes resist him most effectively by going regularly to an altar.

Sometimes we resist the necessity to *think*, to *reflect*, to *consider*, naïvely assuming that it must be all right, in spite of the nagging voice, because everybody is doing it. The advertising industry in America leans heavily on the assumption that the herd instinct is a strong one. The brewers of alcoholic beverage in America know the compulsive power of the thoughtless generalization, "everybody is doing it." In 1959 the United States Brewer's Foundation was told:

Your product is just as essential as bread, and a whole lot more inviting. Beer has eased more troubles, and restored more smiles, than all the comic strips and TV shows in the land. Then the brewers were told to aim their advertising at women, who "are just a nation of sleeping beauties," who need to be told about the "glories of beer."[3]

You may be sure the Brewer's Foundation will not tell anyone that he can become an alcoholic and never drink anything but beer; nor will they tell him that this same narcotic—whether in hard liquor or beer—loosens inhibitions, depresses reflexes, and lowers the thought processes to the level of animal life.

In this age when deliberate pressures are being created to make us conform and to stifle the voice of the warner, it is good to hear one prominent and envied American girl speak her mind on the subject of nonconformity. She was being interviewed on Johnny Carson's *Tonight Show*. Said Mary Ann Mobley, Mississippi's Miss America:

> The man I marry must be a nut. What I mean is that he must be big enough to be "himself" no matter what others are saying or doing or wearing. Few people are willing to pay the price to be themselves, for they are afraid of crowd pressures, or that they will be snubbed if they don't adopt the new style.

We can quash the voice within by stupidly rationalizing, "It must be all right; everybody is doing it."

President Woodrow Wilson, the son of a Presbyterian minister, once made an address on "The Minister and the Community." What he said was pointed toward the minister; it might have been addressed to every person who claims to be a Christian.

> You do not have to *be anything* in particular to be a lawyer. I have been a lawyer and I know. You do not have to *be anything* in particular, except a kindhearted man, perhaps, to be a physician. You do not have to *be anything*, nor undergo any stirring spiritual change, in order to be a merchant. The only profession which consists in *being something* is the ministry of our Lord and Savior—and it does not consist in anything else.[4]

Every Christian has the obligation to *be something*, and the voice of the warner urges us to stop, to consider, to think. Uncritical acceptance of patterns in our lives, the way we've been doing it, deafens the ear of the heart and stifles the voice by which God would make himself known.

Reconciliation

So we have the *argument:* the God who is high is also near; the *charge:* we resist God by devious devices. Now we come to the *offer.* That offer is reconciliation.

George Adam Smith helpfully suggests a translation for verse 13: "Come let us bring the reasoning to a close. . . ."[5] The offer which God is about to make has no rational grounds. It is true. God is high. He is also near. But that does not comprise all the truth about God. There is one more fact: God is love.

We who are on this side of Calvary know better than Isaiah the towering fact of God's love. When we come down to cases, this court day of Isaiah is not a controversy at law. Not really. It is the plea of a rejected lover. This is not an affair of the court; it is an affair of the heart. There is not a shred of rationalism in the offer made: "Though your sins be as scarlet, they shall be as white as snow; though they be red like crimson, they shall be as wool" (Isa. 1:18). This can be nothing but the extravagance of a lover.

Thinly veiled in Isaiah's parable is the fact that each individual is Judah; it is I who stand in the docket, confused and uncertain. With life flowing on like the river, death all around, and the future a great question mark, I need some ground of security, some basis for hope. It cannot be in external things. It must be in the Eternal. And now the voice breaks the bands of time and speaks out of the past to me in the words of Francis Thompson:

> Halts by me that footfall;
> Is my gloom, after all,
> Shade of His hand, outstretched caressingly?

"Ah, fondest, blindest, weakest,
I am He Whom thou seekest!
Thou drawest love from thee, who drawest Me."[6]

Come now, and let us reason together.

Notes

1. Cecil F. Alexander, "All Things Bright and Beautiful," *Baptist Hymnal* (Nashville: The Broadman Press, 1956), p. 8.

2. G. A. Smith, *The Book of Isaiah* (2 vols.; New York: Harper & Row, 1927), I, 5.

3. *The Survey Bulletin* (a publication of the Sunday School Board of the Southern Baptist Convention), February 20, 1959.

4. Peter H. Pleune, *Some to Be Pastors* (Nashville: Abingdon-Cokesbury Press, 1943), p. 43.

5. Smith, *op. cit.*, p. 13.

6. Francis Thompson, "The Hound of Heaven," *The Literature of England,* eds. G. B. Woods *et al.* (2 vols; Chicago: Scott, Foresman and Co., 1941), I, 965.

7

Ballad of the Disappointed Lover

Isaiah 5:1-7

If Isaiah had preached in our time, some of his sermons would have been takeoffs on the current "Top Ten Tunes." As proof we have our Scripture text, which could well be called "The Ballad of the Disappointed Lover." The lyrics strike a familiar theme of Jewish life in the seventh century before Christ: "Now will I sing to my well-beloved a song of my beloved touching his vineyard." That may not sound romantic to us; it was the height of romanticism to Isaiah's hearers.

Were we to anticipate, we would expect the song to break out in a rapturous celebration of the vineyard and its virtues, all of which would serve as a transparent guise for extolling the delights of a lover. Our expectations are not disappointed. The first stanza describes the meticulous care with which this beloved cared for a vineyard: "He digged it and cleared it of stones, and planted it with choice vines; he built a watchtower in the midst of it, and hewed out a wine vat in it" (v. 2). The art here is not subtle at all; it is what we expect. Even the floating notes of the dulcimer and the flute are expected.

But what we do not expect is the last line in the first stanza of the ballad: "And he looked for it to yield grapes, And it brought forth—stinking grapes!" (cf. v. 2).

On this surprise note the first stanza comes to a close.

Verse two is an appeal to the hearers. Their sense of fair play is called up: "Judge . . . between me and my vineyard" (RSV). The lapse into the personal pronoun confirms our dawning surmise that here is no fiction; this is the grief of a disappointed lover. The only question is who is the lover? He asks plaintively: "Why did it yield wild grapes?" Or in an expanded form: "Why did this love affair go so wrong?"

The interlude between verses two and three modulates into a minor key. The lilting airs of the dulcimer and flute give way to the throbbing beat of the viol and the plaintive wail of the oboe. A cloud has passed over. There is a new mood, a mood of anger and outrage. The words are pungent, direct:

> I'll make an end of it;
>> unpruned, unweeded,
> It shall be overgrown
>> with thorns and thistles (cf. v. 6).

The music moves to a *pianissimo* now. We can hear both the plaintive minors of the dirge and the lyric airs of the love song. We are about to discover the identity of this disappointed lover:

> For the vineyard of the Lord of hosts
>> is the house of Israel,
> and the men of Judah
>> are his pleasant planting;
> and he looked for justice,
>> but behold, bloodshed;
> for righteousness,
>> but behold, a cry! (v. 7, RSV).

And so the Ballad of the Disappointed Lover concludes.

In this ballad is an abbreviated, romanticized version of the whole history of Israel up to Isaiah's time. The fundamental fact of Israel's history as Isaiah saw it was the fact of providence. From the earliest moment on, the history of Israel could best be understood in recognition of the eternal Father's special interest and in the response Israel made to that interest. So although this ballad is on the theme of a disappointed lover, it can better be understood if we see it as a ballad on the ways of providence and men. Implicit in the ballad are three identifiable thoughts: providence defined, providence abused, and providence asserted.

Providence Defined

If you look in the ballad for a definition of providence, or even for the word itself, you will be disappointed. It is not there, not explicitly. But the thought is there lying quietly underneath it all. What is providence? It is a way of *looking* at things, looking back over the shoulder. When Isaiah is talking about all that the husbandman had done for his vineyard, you recognize that he is talking about something more than a garden. As a matter of fact, Isaiah is looking back over his shoulder down the long road over which Israel has come.

This road begins in Ur of the Chaldees. Abram is the first traveler. The road runs through Haran, Bethel, by the Cave of Machpelah (where Sarah was buried), down to Egypt, back to Canaan. Successive generations travel this road until we come to a long detour in Egypt. This detour lasts 430 years.

The next significant person is Moses. Here the road leads out of Egypt, through the wilderness of Sinai, on to Canaan. Traveling the road are such notables as Joshua, David, Solomon, Uzziah.

The most noteworthy thing about that long journey is (and this can best be seen looking back over the way we have come) that an unseen hand and an invisible presence has made the long journey, too.

That mysterious fact is called providence. If you want to define it, you can say that it is a way of *looking* at things. It is to confess:

"Here I raise mine Ebenezer; Hither by thy help I've come."
How are we looking at things?

Consider. The lines have fallen in pleasant places for you. You are comfortably situated, enjoy a reasonable degree of good health, have a minimum of serious conflicts and a maximum of good things. Who is responsible for all this?

Two Ways

There are probably only two ways of looking at it. You may say, "Look what I've done! In these ten, twenty, thirty years since entering adult life, I've erected a sheltering roof for me and my loved ones, developed a certain style of life, carved out a little chunk of the American pie. It's been hard work; I bear some scars; I've paid the price. But now it's mine, and I can settle back to enjoy a little of the comfort and the leisure I've earned." That's one way of looking at things.

The other way is to say something like this: "I don't deserve all the wonderful things that have come to me. In the first place, I was given my ancestry, my physical and cultural heritage. My partner in marriage is more than I deserve. Our children are normal (or nearly so, I would like to believe) and they are a blessing no amount of money can buy. We have our little problems and once in a while a heartache, but they are really nothing. Our sheltering roof, my career, the family, my country, my church—these are things given me, not earned. When I come to worship and put my offering in the plate, I'm not trying to pay off or buy off. I'm just saying thank you for all the blessings!"

That is another way of looking at things. This way accepts providence as a fact of life.

Isaiah looked over his shoulder down the long road of the past, and he was convinced that providence was a fact. That assumption, that belief in divine guidance, underlies his Ballad of the Disappointed Lover.

Providence Abused

The point of the ballad is that Israel never wholeheartedly accepted providence as a way of looking at things. The little beachhead of civilization which they had established in Canaan they regarded as their own to do with as they pleased.

They pleased to have a king, so they crowned one.

They pleased to worship in groves and shrines, so they built them.

They pleased to bow down before idols, so they practiced idolatry.

They pleased to practice sexual looseness as a worship rite, so they practiced immorality in the name of religion.

They pleased to rob and defraud each other, so they bribed their priests and their judges.

They pleased to disregard their prophets, so they snubbed them or ignored them, and sometimes they killed them.

That is the way Israel responded to providence.

But what of us? How do we respond to providence?

We have already seen the two fundamental responses reflected in our way of looking at things. But beyond our way of looking at things is an attitude toward the Heavenly Father. It is this attitude which concerns us now.

If we respond to providence acceptably, we will have an attitude of *responsible cooperation*. We will recognize that within certain limits we do have a choice to make, and we must make it affirmatively. Our attitude is one of affirmation. We say yes! to him in whom we live, move, and have our being. Not just once, but over and over, every day.

Each of us must make a choice. God gave us that power, and he will not revoke it. As Markham puts it:

> I will leave man to make the fateful guess,
> Will leave him torn between the No and Yes,

Leave him unresting till he rests in Me,
Drawn upward by the choice that makes him free—
Leave him in tragic loneliness to choose,
With all in life to win or all to lose.[1]

The contrasting attitude is that of *irresponsible refusal,* and in this attitude we find ourselves at times and the vast majority most of the time.

Sometimes it is just indifference. "So they're having a hard time finding teachers! Well, I wish 'em luck." The only kind of attitude which can rise above the downward pull of indifference and resist the comfort of sinking into the faceless crowd is one which recognizes a debt to the Father, to others, to society. Indifference is a form of irresponsibility, and it is not Christian. Studdert-Kennedy tells us just how unchristian it is:

When Jesus came to Golgotha, they hanged him on a tree,
They drove great nails through hands and feet, and made a
    Calvary;
They crowned him with a crown of thorns: red were his
    wound and deep—
For those were crude and cruel days, and human flesh was
    cheap.

When Jesus came to Birmingham, we merely passed him by;
We wouldn't hurt a hair of him; we only let him die.
For men had grown more tender; they would not give him
    pain—
They merely passed on down the street and left him in the rain.

Still Jesus cried, "Forgive them, for they know not what they
    do."
And still it rained the winter rain that drenched him through
    and through.
The crowds went home and left the street, with not a soul
    to see,
That Jesus crouched against a wall, and cried for Calvary.[2]

Sometimes our irresponsibility is more aggressive than that; we actually thrust any suggestion of responsibility from us. It is not always easy to admit our involvement. When the Lord God went walking and searching in the cool of the evening and found Eve's sin out, Eve thrust her responsibility away. "The serpent gave to me, and I ate." Adam learned the game from her, for he said, "The woman gave me, and I ate." And I suppose, if the story had carried on, the serpent would have said, "You put me out of heaven, and here were these two innocents just waiting for someone to come along and teach them how to be wrongdoers." They were all thrusting the final responsibility onto God.

But of course, the responsibility is ours. If we accept that and work within the limitations given, providence and the stars in their courses are on our side.

Usually, however, the vast majority of us doesn't think that far ahead. We presume that all we have we deserve; it never occurs to us that God might want us to be something and to do something beyond ourselves.

Providence Asserted

In the ballad, the husbandman exercises an admirable restraint up to a point. Then, there is the awesome, even frightening, picture of a thoroughly aroused farmer making havoc out of the very thing into which he had put so much thought and care. It can be terrifying if you let it sink in:

> I will remove its hedge,
>   and it shall be devoured;
> I will break down its wall,
>   and it shall be trampled down.
> I will make it a waste;
>   it shall not be pruned or hoed,
>   and briers and thorns shall grow up (vv. 5-6, RSV).

What is Isaiah saying? That God indulges well beyond the limits of propriety but that once he is aroused, his wrath is also well beyond the limits of propriety? That he is like an easygoing parent who waits too long and who then disciplines too much?

We would make a serious mistake if we read human foibles into the divine character. That is not the point, not at all. What Isaiah is saying in his Ballard of the Disappointed Lover is that there is a limit beyond which we go only at our own peril, that the limit is not specifically defined.

> Oh, where is that mysterious bourne
>   By which each path is crossed,
> Beyond which God himself hath sworn
>   That he who goes is lost?
>
> How long may man go on in sin,
>   How long will God forbear?
> Where does hope end, and where begins
>   The confines of despair?
>
> The answer from the skies is sent,
>   Ye who from God depart:
> While it is yet Today, repent,
>   And harden not your heart.[3]

"While it is yet today, repent."

That is the point. Isaiah's ballad was not written to entertain; it was written to warn and to encourage—to warn against abusing providence by an attitude of indifference, to encourage a responsible cooperation with the purposes of God, using all we have in our control, under him.

A few years ago, as we traveled through Scottish border country, our guide, who loved every stone of his native Scotland and seemed to know her every story, pointed out an unusual landmark. It was a rough tower built on a low-lying hill. It is called "Repentance Tower." It was built several hundred years ago by a border thief who came to have a profound and deep change in his life. First, he built his "Repentance Tower"; then he spent the remaining years doing good and trying to atone for the mischief of his earlier days.

The object of this Ballad of the Disappointed Lover is to move us to build here in this moment our own Repentance Towers, then to use our remaining days trying to do good and to serve the Saviour who redeems us from our sins.

Notes

1. Edwin Markham, "The Testing," *Masterpieces* . . ., p. 61.
2. G. A. Studdert-Kennedy, "Indifference," *Masterpieces* . . ., p. 383.
3. Quoted to author personally by Fred M. Wood.

8

A Tale of Two Fathers

Isaiah 7:1-16

Jerusalem, her king, and her citizens were jittery. Although the plain citizen could not know the precise details, it was a dull one who did not sense the air of impending calamity.

The king's foreign office was a beehive. Diplomats from their foreign posts scurried in and out looking distracted and harried. Informed sources identified these diplomats as being from Damascus in Syria, Samaria in Israel, and Nineveh of Assyria. It was apparent to all that something big was about to break.

The tension mounted still higher when it became known that the king himself, with a retinue of his most trusted advisers, had gone to inspect the city's water works. This seemed to indicate either a siege or invasion. The astute began laying by extra stores.

Isaiah the prophet was one of the more astute, but his interest was not in laying by an extra supply of grocery staples. It was far more vital than that. His interest lay in saving both his king and his country. but even more personal, in scotching his own son's future.

Isaiah's private sources filled in the picture of the dilemma facing Ahaz the king. Reson of Damascus and Pekah of Samaria were even then gathering on his northern border. But the country

itself was divided. Some nurtured a vivid memory of Uzziah—
now dead six years—and fondly opined that no such coalition
would have dared war in his day. To them, Ahaz was a pale
shadow of Davidic greatness. They held Ahaz in contempt.

There were others, however, who took a more realistic view
of things. They recognized that international conditions had
changed since Uzziah's time. They knew that the balance of
Assyrian and Egyptian power hunger was delicate and deadly,
that this balance had been upset in recent months, that the
impending invasion was vitally related to these facts. To them,
the only practical step was to send out an urgent appeal to old
Tiglath-pileser, the Assyrian war-horse, offering to make Judah
a satellite and a captive people.

Between these two conflicting segments of thought—the roman-
ticists who condemned Ahaz and lived in past glory, and the
pragmatists who commended Ahaz and lived only for the present
status quo—Ahaz was caught. No matter what his move, some
would call it an evidence of weakness, a confession of unfitness
for his Davidic heritage.

To the harassed king, then, came the prophet Isaiah, out to
the water works. He came only to help. But the encounter was
not all that Isaiah had hoped for. Ahaz was defensive, hostile,
and cagey. The conversation ends with a sign which Ahaz could
only interpret as ominous, but in which the church has found
a blessed intimation of her coming Redeemer.

This, then, is the scene in which is set the tale of the two
fathers. As you may already have gathered, one of these fathers
is Isaiah the prophet. The other is Ahaz, the king. These two
fathers will serve as stack-poles around which we gather our
thoughts. If you think it strange that I have chosen this setting
in which stress and tension are so prominent a feature, I would
simply comment that what a father is and does probably comes
under no more severe test than when under extreme pressure.

Isaiah and His Son

I wonder if it struck you, as it did me when I read the passage again, that it seems a little strange that Isaiah should think it pleasing to God for him to take along his young son on such an important encounter. The natural thing to think is that Isaiah would need to do just the opposite, that the stakes were so high he could ill afford to risk any distraction. Why would Isaiah include his young son in this dramatic and important venture?

We must be cautious here that we do not read too much into this rather obscure fact. Some scholars tell us that Isaiah the prophet took his son along to be a kind of walking parable, a warning to the king. They remind us that, after all, the prophet's son was named Shear-jashub, which means a "remnant shall remain." It may have been a psychological trick, a subliminal playing with the fears of the king.

It further occurs to me (and I admit I may be reading something into the story here) that Isaiah could have had a far more personal reason for taking along his young son. Isaiah, you will remember, was a *father*. He knew that time was his enemy, that whatever values and insight his young son had a decade hence would be the bloom of a present husbandry. Could it be that Isaiah, the father, wanted his son to learn a little history in the making? to observe firsthand the challenge of faith?

You will recall the essential features of that encounter. Isaiah, taking his young son Shear-jashub with him, goes out to the king as he inspects the city's water system. He advises the king that the gathering army on his northern border is but the smoking wisp of two burnt-out stumps. To be afraid of them is to fear a phantom. Isaiah urges Ahaz to stand pat: "If you don't have faith, you will have no future." In the back of both men's minds is the proposal to call on the ruthless Tiglath-pileser for help. There is no mention of that in the conversation reported. They didn't need to speak of it; both men were thinking it. Isaiah intimates that such a decision would be the height of folly, a betrayal of the heritage of David's faith.

Isaiah pushes his case by daring to offer the king any sign he might ask. Here Isaiah put his own reputation as a prophet squarely on the line. Suppose Ahaz should ask for a sign he could not produce? Then what? But Isaiah took that risk.

It turned out to be a needless risk. Ahaz may have already made his overtures to this foreign oppressor. He would not ask a sign, for if Isaiah produced it, then he could do only what Isaiah might say. The king was not ready for that. He declined to ask a sign in a show of false piety.

Then Isaiah makes a move that has both boldness and stature. "Very well," he says. "I'll not give you an immediate sign; I'll give you a sign which you will live to see fulfilled. A young woman of marriageable age will soon conceive and bear a son, and his name will be called Immanu-El (God with us). Curds and honey will he eat. And before he is old enough to know the good and refuse the evil (before he is twelve years old) the nations which you grovel before will be forsaken. And the king of Assyria will inflict upon your own land a desolation such as Judah has not known since Ephraim departed Judah" (cf. vv. 14-17).

Isaiah may have wanted to teach his son that a father has work to do. Somehow, it seems, we have come upon a generation that has not seen the connection between work and fatherhood. Before a boy takes the risk of fatherhood with a girl, it might be well to ask whether or not he is prepared to buy milk for the baby. If a boy does not ask such a question, it may not be all his fault.

Perhaps his father must pick up part of the burden of this gap in his son's thinking. The father has financed the boy in the basic things—food, shelter, clothes. He has paid his expenses at school. He has given him a car to drive and paid for the gasoline. He has made it possible for this boy to be with his girl in the most convenient and comfortable ways imaginable. The boy gets the idea that these things "just come." He has never had to work for any of them. Further, he has never seen his father at work; he just knows Dad is away from home a lot of the time.

Who is to blame if the boy becomes a father before he can buy milk for the baby? Certainly the boy. But altogether? Perhaps Isaiah wanted his boy to see him at work!

The father can become a nonentity in family life. If he is addicted to his work—a slave—his continued absence from home at all vital times imposes a terrible burden upon his wife. She must teach her sons what she cannot teach them: how to be a man! And all the while, the siblings miss the comfort and the security of the father-figure in their lives. The boy will substitute his "gang"; the girl will devise some way to get the attention and affection of her father, even if it means using her body as a weapon.

Then again, Isaiah may have wanted to teach young Shear-jashub that life simply cannot be wrapped up in a neat little package, bound with a ribbon, and set off by a bow. There are always some ragged, frayed edges hanging out somewhere. Something we thought was nailed down is always getting loose. If you want life to be as neat as an algebraic formula, you want too much. Trying to get it reduced to its simplest terms will get you before you get the answer.

Ahaz had a neat answer all worked out for his little country's crisis. The only trouble was in the delayed repayment plan. Perhaps Isaiah wanted his son to learn that a vital faith is better than pat answers, flexibility better than rigidity, obedience better than enlightened self-interest.

Carl Sandburg in these lines imagines a father speaking to a son nearing manhood:

"Life is hard; be steel; be a rock."
And this might stand him for the storms
and serve him for humdrum and monotony
and guide him amid sudden betrayals
and tighten him for slack moments.
. . . .
"Life is a soft loam; be gentle; go easy."
And this too might serve him.
. . . .
The growth of a frail flower in a path up
has sometimes shattered and split a rock.
A tough will counts. So does desire.
. . . .
Tell him too much money has killed men
and left them dead years before burial:
. . . .
Tell him time as stuff can be wasted.
Tell him to be a fool every so often.[1]

Perhaps Isaiah was conducting a dialogue like that with his son in this encounter with his king.

Isaiah may have chosen to include his son in this vital conversation with Ahaz the king as a means of clueing Shear-jashub on the nature of faith. Do you remember that sentence of Isaiah's to Ahaz? "If you have no faith, you will have no future" (v. 9). Or as the Scottish preachers put it: "If you have no *faith*, you will have no *staith*." What is Isaiah saying here?

Ahaz had a neat little solution all worked out. He would call on Tiglath-pileser of Assyria, become a satellite in his orbit of influence, and depend on this powerful pagan king to deliver him from his enemy. Ahaz was looking for some kind of tangible, external arrangement to support him. His security rested on external things.

Could it be that Isaiah wanted his son to learn that faith sometimes has nothing but invisible supports, a kind of inside intuition, a certainty that to be right is better than to be wrong and to be safe? Perhaps Isaiah was trying to show his son in this one little capsule of time how wrong it is to think only of "playing it safe."

Perhaps Isaiah was looking down the corridor of the years. He would no longer be around. Isaiah believed that Judah might well be in eclipse, or nearly so. Shear-jashub might be in captivity in a foreign land. Everything external would be swept away. Would he have the staying power for it? Could he stand then?

Isaiah chose this way to teach his son these fundamental lessons about life.

Ahaz and His Sons

We need not spend much time with Ahaz.

George Adam Smith says that the name "Immanuel" indicates that Isaiah's predicted Saviour is of the Davidic line, that he will be the fulfilment of the grandest Davidic hopes. Perhaps Ahaz listened hard when Isaiah said that; Isaiah was talking about the king's son! But Ahaz is smitten by the next words of Isaiah: "Curds and honey will he eat." Says Dr. Smith:

Curds and honey are the food of privation, the food of a people, whose land depopulated by the enemy, has been turned into pasture. Before this Child shall arrive at years of discretion . . . the Lord himself will have laid waste Judah.[2]

Isaiah was warning that Ahaz, in his very efforts to preserve what he thought was important, might lose it all. It might be that how we play the game is more important than anything else.

I heard Dr. Wayne Oates of our Southern Baptist seminary speaking privately to a small group in Louisville. One of the top men in his field in America today, author of several books, Dr. Oates said:

There was a time when I could not say in a group what I am about to say. But I have come to accept my own history and appreciate it—draw strength from it. Neither my father nor my mother had a first grade education. There was little they could give me. But of what they did have, they gave their best, and whatever I am today, they are a part of it. I have drawn from them, and they pushed me out beyond their limitations.

That is what I mean by *how* we play the game. There is something more than winning; that something more is playing the game with integrity, courage, and faith.

I said earlier that in this encounter between Ahaz and Isaiah a bright ray is struck which the church has taken as an intimation of the coming of her Redeemer. It is the word on the birth of Immanuel. It was Matthew who saw in this word of Isaiah its fulfilment in the Christmas story. It is the story of the birth of Jesus, who came to take us by the hand and heart to lead us back to him. When this Jesus came to be a man, he would teach his disciples about God and how to pray to him, saying: "Our Father, which art in heaven. . . ." Certainly Jesus was not thinking of a father like Ahaz. Perhaps it was a father like Isaiah, or his own father, Joseph, from whom he had learned what it was to be loved, accepted, and encouraged to live life to the full.

So here we have the story of two fathers—one a prophet, the other a king. What made the difference in them? Was it not that one was a man of faith?

Isaiah lived on yonder side of Immanuel; he saw him only in prospect. We have the luminous reality, and he will help us to become the fathers we yearn to be. We, who are only children of the Heavenly Father, can have his help.

> Last night my little boy confessed to me
> Some childish wrong;
> And kneeling at my knee,

He prayed with tears—
"Dear God, make me a man
Like Daddy—wise and strong;
I know you can."

Then while he slept
I knelt beside his bed,
Confessed my sins,
And prayed with low-bowed head.
"O God, make me a child
Like my child here—
Pure, guileless,
Trusting Thee with faith sincere.[3]

Notes

1. Carl Sandburg, *The People, Yes* (New York: Harcourt, Brace and Company, 1936), poem number 9, p. 18.
2. Smith, *op. cit.*, p. 18.
3. Andrew Gillies, "Two Prayers," *Masterpieces* . . ., p. 383.

9

Food for the Fed Up

Isaiah 55

You may recall the essential outline of Ernest Hemingway's Pulitzer prize-winning novel, *Old Man and the Sea*. The ancient fisherman has been outmoded by the new fishing methods, but he stoutly maintains his own sense of worth by a stubborn pursuit of the old ways. On this particular trip the old man ties into a leviathan and senses that here is the catch of his life.

The giant fish pulls his boat around like a bobbing chip, but the old man fights his protagonist of the deep. The struggle continues through several days and nights. The fish is wounded and tires; its blood draws the sharks. The old man is delirious with exposure and fatigue, but instinct in him fights on. Finally, life is gone at the deep end of his tackle, and he sets himself the task of beaching his catch. But when he finally draws in his line, he has nothing but a skeleton. The sharks have eaten his fish. The old man, though victor, is beaten.

Was this Hemingway's confession of a collapse of faith and meaning in life? I wondered.

Early in July, 1961, I read that Hemingway, living out in Ketchum, Idaho, had shot himself. I was not too surprised at the news; but what was Hemingway—a man who had lived in America, Paris, Cuba, and Africa—doing in Idaho?

In an article that appeared recently in the *National Observer* my question was answered. Hunter Thompson had wondered the same thing and went to Ketchum to find out. This, in part, is what he discovered:

> Ketchum was perhaps the only place in his world that had not changed radically. . . . Europe had been completely transformed, Africa was in the process of drastic upheaval, and finally even Cuba blew up around him like a volcano. . . .
> Only Ketchum seemed unchanged, and it was here that he decided to dig in.

But even Ketchum could not offer asylum to an old man whose youthful strength had become aging rigidity. The trouble with Hemingway was not coming from the outside; it was inside. And Thompson writes on:

> Perhaps he found what he came here for, but the odds are huge that he didn't. He was an old, sick, and very troubled man, and the illusion of peace and contentment was not enough for him—not even when his friends came up from Cuba and played bullfight with him in the Tram. So finally, and for what he must have thought the best of reasons, he ended it with a shotgun.[1]

I mention Ernest Hemingway and his tumble into the abyss of meaninglessness not just because it is a dramatic human-interest story, but because he seems to symbolize something that is happening in the lifetime of those now living. There seems to be a prevailing sentiment of indifference (at best) and cynicism (at worst). The old answers simply do not speak to the new questions. We have a generation that seems to be fed up on the old diet, but starving for want of a nourishing substitute.

I have taken the parable Isaiah told of food for the fed up as a scriptural foundation for our thought.

As a method of procedure let me suggest the clinical approach.

We will examine the symptoms, make a diagnosis, prescribe a remedy. We will follow the prophet.

The Symptoms

The prophet looks beyond the apparent to the real. The apparent is a gloss of prosperity and success. In Babylon the Jewish nation had directed its splendid gifts of insight, imagination, and tenacity to the commerce of that great city. It was in Babylon that Judah became a trader. There she labored and prospered, settling down by the streams of Babylon that were no longer bitter with her tears. To the superficial observer, the Jews had made an excellent adjustment.

But to the prophet, whose eye saw beyond the shell to the core, it was apparent that his countrymen were miserably unhappy. They could not leave well enough alone; they had to have something better. They were on a bitter treadmill—never content.

To such a generation the prophet addressed his parable, couched in incisive questions: "Why do you spend money for that which is not bread? Why do you work for that which cannot satisfy?" (vv. 2, RSV). Their souls had the lean and hungry look.

Could it be that these questions come hauntingly out of the past to taunt us? Even the symptoms are very much the same. Any man or woman who has been grinding out life on the millstone of job or career for fifteen or twenty years will recognize the mood reflected in the passage below, written by one who had personally experienced the whirl of modern commerce:

And they said to me, "Go to now—let us have a fight." And I said to them, "But what are we fighting about and what are we fighting for?"

And they said to me, "Oh, we are fighting about first one thing and then the other."

And I said, "But what are we fighting for?"

And I heard only a buzzing among them. A few giggles punctured the buzzing.

So—I went away and climbed a great high hill and looked at the blinking neon signs across a great wide river on which hovered the commerce of the nations.

Then I heard the Lord say: "Do you want to know what the fighting is for? I will tell you: Two yards of sackcloth, a bucket of ashes, and a quart of gall. The sackcloth and ashes will be to those who still can feel enough after the fight to sense its futility and repent. The quart of gall will be for those who can no longer feel either for themselves or for others and can taste only that which is bitter.[2]

Another Bench Mark

But futility is not the only bench mark of our time. Another, seen most often by the medical practitioner, is physical malfunction. One medical man, Dr. W. W. Bauer, spoke about this new malfunction five years ago at a meeting of the American Public Health Association. The newspaper reported the speech:

"Surrounded by problems, threats and confusions, fearful of impending chaos, man strives for serenity—and fails to find it." Then he went on to speak of the impact of this emotional unrest on the physical body, which helps produce ulcers, colitis, high blood pressure, hardening of the arteries, heart attacks, strokes, allergies and many other conditions.

Dr. Bauer noted that many people are attempting to control their tensions by gobbling aspirin, sleeping pills, pep pills and tranquillizers. But in other cases, man seeks refuge from intolerable stresses in narcotics, alcoholism, neuroticism, divorce, the mad search for pleasure and the cynical philosophy of making friends and influencing people.[3]

For many Americans, life has gotten to be nothing more than one big headache, on which (according to the *Wall Street Journal*) we spent $200 million in a recent year trying to get some temporary relief.

Like the generation to which the prophet spoke his parable, we spend ourselves on that which satisfieth not.

Diagnosis

Description of symptoms is itself an exercise in futility. We must take the next clinical step; we must make a diagnosis. The prophet made a diagnosis for his time. It was *leanness of soul.* In the mad whirl of Babylon, in the struggle to carve a little piece of the economic pie for themselves, they had forgotten their own essence. For man is more than a body, and it takes more than material things to satisfy him. Man is a living soul.

Is it any different today?

Every age has its own "worldview," as the Germans call it, its own perception of reality, its own idea of how things "stack up." One need not be very clever to find clues that indicate the character of an age.

Someone has found a clue to understanding the Western world in the dances of the past three centuries. In the eighteenth century it was the minuet, a precise, restricted, formal dance step. That reflected the mood of a century when kings still reigned and human knowledge ran smoothly in the bounds of an orderly world.

The nineteenth century brought in the waltz. This new style was less inhibited, less formal. The dance seemed to reflect a new approach to knowledge. This was the century of Darwin, Marx, Freud, and Nietzsche, men who brought new understanding in the fields of biology, economics, psychology, and philosophy. It was an adventuresome sounding of old intellectual harbors.

The twentieth century came cascading in to the accompaniment of jazz. From the Charleston of the twenties to the Big Apple, the Twist, the Lindy Hop of the sixties, all is a riot of motion. Some is coordinated, some not, but it all reflects a century of the broken atom, the space rocket, the electronic brain, and the automated assembly line. The bouncy, nervous dance of our generation has caught up the roiled waters of our own pyschic unrest.

What is at bottom of the jerky, frenetic, meaningless motion of our age? Is this but the surface expression of a deeper unrest? Some say so.

Duke McCall, in a recent impromptu address on theological education, reproduced the gist of an analysis of our age given by a visiting speaker on the seminary campus. This speaker divided the last seventeen hundred years of Western history into three eras. The first, he said, was the era of the *Christian mind*. It began about the fourth century A.D. and continued through the seventeenth. In this era, the ultimate reality was God, and the requirements for man were set forth in the Christian revelation, the Bible. Nature was unintelligible. Scientists of this era thought the earth was flat and fixed, that the body had four primary fluids, and so forth.

The second era he called the *modern mind*. In this era, which began about 1800 and continued until World War II, the assumption was that reality was orderly, that nature could be understood and her secrets unraveled, that ultimate reality was the material. This eased God out, except perhaps as an impersonal First Cause. God was denuded of personality.

The third and present era, this speaker said, could be called the *post-modern mind*. Scientists are no longer sure that nature is altogether predictable. The nucleus of the atom is fluid rather than fixed, in motion rather than stable. Nor is man certain that his intelligence altogether corresponds with reality. The question is now being asked earnestly whether or not man is really capable of understanding this universe in which he lives. The post-modern mind has put a question mark behind all the undergirding assumptions of knowledge up to this point.

There seems to be some correspondence between the frenzied motion of the jitterbug and this pervading uneasiness which comes from the best intellectual circles. We are not sure about anything. Everything we had nailed down is coming loose. This could easily explain the sex revolution of our day. It may be the clue to understanding the contradiction of historic highs in membership of our churches and historic lows in moral power. If we cannot be sure that geometric axioms are true, then we cannot be sure that the church is true, either.

This, it seems to me, may explain the leanness of soul in our day.

Remedy

We have the diagnosis. What of the remedy?

I must admit that this question hit me hard as I began to put these thoughts down on paper. Then I remembered a man whose whole structure of spiritual, theological, and philosophical presuppositions came under the severest possible attack. His name was Dietrich Bonhoeffer. He was a university professor when Hitler began his rise to power. Bonhoeffer, though quite a young man, saw where Hitler was moving and was one of the first to oppose him. Eventually he was put in prison, and ironically, the day before the allied forces overran Flossenburg Prison, he was put to death.

In the course of those two years in prison, Bonhoeffer wrote a series of letters to friends outside. In those letters and papers, since gathered together and edited in a book, Bonhoeffer sees his own neat little world fall apart. Everything he had counted on crumbles: his theology, the nature of reality, the trustworthiness of the Bible, even the God who hides himself—particularly from a man in prison. What would such a man have to say when his own world was so shattered?

I picked up a dog-eared copy of his letters and journals and began to read some of those lines again. In one passage Bonhoeffer makes a grand survey of various systems of theological thought, examines their strength and weakness, gives his own appraisal, moves on to the next. Finally, he comes to say that this is not a time to argue or structure formal ways of thought; this is a time to turn to Christ. Here we have something we can understand. Here is a person, and in this person who lived, suffered, died, was buried, and rose again we have a clue for our understanding of God. A little later he writes this luminous passage:

. . . For the Christian it is essential to have a hope that is based on solid foundations. However potent a force illusion may be, the influence of a sure and certain hope is infinitely greater, and the lives of those who possess it are invincible. Christ our hope—this Pauline formula is our life's inspiration.[4]

No one can deny a life. God has given us such a life in Jesus. We may have difficulty committing ourselves to Jesus. But he is our hope; he is the remedy; he is the changeless amidst the changing.

A scrubwoman in London was taken sick. Her friends made it possible for her to go to the hospital. While she was convalescing there, she went up and down the corridor becoming acquainted with other patients. Across the hall from her was a boy, twelve years old, redheaded, freckle-faced. She and he talked every day. Then one morning she was awakened early by commotion in the hall, and before long the boy's mother came in to say to the scrubwoman: "The doctors say Johnny has about ten minutes to live. Won't you say something to him?"

That was a hard assignment. But this London scrubwoman, with the courage of a great Christian, walked quietly across the hall and sat down beside Johnny. She took his thin hand in her calloused palms and looked at him. Quietly, she said: "Listen, Johnny. God made you. God loves you. God sent his Son to save you. God wants you to come home to live with him."

The little fellow turned his eyes weakly toward his older friend, and said in a whisper barely audible: "Say it again."

Quietly she repeated the same words: "God made you. God loves you. God sent his Son to save you. God wants you to come home to live with him."

Johnny looked into the calm face of his friend and said, "Tell God, Thank you."

That is food for the fed up, or the knocked down, or the dragged out.

Notes

1. Hunter Thompson, "What Lured Hemingway to Ketchum," *National Observer*, III (May 25, 1964), 13.

2. Wayne Oates, *The Revelation of God in Human Suffering* (Philadelphia: Westminster Press, 1959), p. 72.

3. John Troan, "Religion Urged for Jittery Americans," *Knoxville News-Sentinel*, October 22, 1959.

4. Dietrich Bonhoeffer, *Letters and Papers from Prison* (London: Collins Clear-Type Press, Fontana Books, 1959), cf. pp. 108, 110, 126. Copyright held by S. C. M. Press, 1953.

10

The Years of the Locusts

Joel 2:21-25

Have you ever had the unsettling experience of losing time—a day, perhaps, or a week, or a year?

R. Benjamin West, pastor of the influential Hillyer Memorial Christian Church of Raleigh, North Carolina, tells about such a loss in his little book, *Light Beyond Shadow*. It is an intensely personal book describing his period of mental illness. The author recounts his first painful return to the real world after several months of severe withdrawal:

. . . Alarmed, I asked myself: "Why do I feel so strange? A new freshness and an old tiredness—and both at the same time. Why do I feel so old? By George, I can't even remember my own age! I was born in 1916. But what year is this? How long did I sleep, anyhow? For hours? Days? Or could it have been years?"[1]

That is one way of losing time, and a frightening way. But there are other, more frightening ways.

I had a friend who became a Christian after his eightieth birthday. Every time I went to see him, his conversation included a wistful reference to the lost years of his life. They were years lost to joy, peace, and service to Christ. They were years that the locusts had eaten.

Some years ago when I first came to be pastor of the congregation I now serve, I was asked to visit a wonderful little woman who was desperately ill with a heart disease. She had been ill for ten years. I did not know her long until I stood over her casket. In those weeks just before she died, she wrote me a letter filled with pathos and regret. It was a confession of her feeling of lost time. She had refused to teach and witness in the years of her strength. She was haunted by the years that the locusts had eaten.

The little book of Joel was written in the midst of national turmoil. The prophet, about whom we know precious little, had a burning conviction that the natural castastrophes which had settled upon land and people were but the heavy hand of God's judgment. The prophet saw the legend "Ichabod"—"the glory is departed"—writ large across the face of the nation. One half of the seventy-three verses in the book are devoted to this message of doom. But in the midst of his writings, the mood of the prophets shifts. He is gripped in a kind of prophetic ecstasy and sees the possibility of restoration for his little nation. It is in this happier frame that Joel gives us the beautiful and meaningful promise of our text: "I will restore the years that the locusts have eaten" (2:25).

As I meditated upon this message from God's Word, seeking some particular meaning for those who are in any way beginning anew, Joel's lovely promise kept recurring like a haunting theme. In the midst of old failures what better truth could undergird our lives at the threshold of a new beginning than this: "I will restore the years the locusts have eaten"?

Embraced in this engaging little metaphor are great Bible truths which may be expressed in three simple sentences.

God's eye is on the sparrow.

God's hand is in the storm.

God's grace covers our sin.

God's Eye Is on the Sparrow

This word of Joel was prompted by a memorable disaster of nature. Judah was devasted by an invasion of locusts. The prophet describes it very early in his writing: "That which the palmerworm hath left hath the locust eaten; and that which the locust hath left the cankerworm hath eaten; and that which the cankerworm hath left hath the caterpillar eaten" (1:4). Here was distress enough to paralyze the whole of life. The markets and shops in the villages of the countryside were idle. The shelves were empty. Food was scarce. The cattle were dying for want of pasture and water. The ground was stripped bare. Organized society had collapsed. Temple services were suspended. Life was on its simplest, most primitive level.

To the Jews of Judah and Jerusalem, nature had shown a frightening, unfriendly face. Some cursed nature. Others cursed the weather, or their luck, or the locusts. The land was in the grip of despair. There was a deadly want of faith.

It is fairly easy to believe in God's goodness when things are going well for us. We settle into a comfortable routine and observe that God "helps those who help themselves" while "idlers come to grief." But then life gets unstrung, gives us the back of the hand, and faith is hard to come by. It is not difficult to understand the mood of Job's wife, who counseled: "Curse God and die."

You have to think about it a while before it dawns on you that even this reaction has behind it a religious assumption. The assumption is that God is good and God knows. When life does go sour on us and we are tempted to become cynical, it is good to remember that even the instinct to cynicism is prompted by the unspoken assumption that God's eye is on the sparrow. God knows; we want to think God cares.

One of the sweetest word pictures Jesus ever painted of the

Heavenly Father is this: "Are not two sparrows sold for a farthing? and one of them shall not fall on the ground without your Father. Fear ye not therefore, ye are of more value than many sparrows" (Matt. 10:29, 31).

A poet has taken that strand of thought, weaving it with the shuttle of imagination into a conversation, overheard in an orchard:

> Said the Robin to the Sparrow,
>   "I would really like to know
> Why these anxious human beings
> Rush around and worry so."
>
> Said the Sparrow to the Robin,
>   "I think that it must be
> They have no Heavenly Father
> Such as watches you and me."[2]

But there remain the locusts, and we must look elsewhere for an explanation.

God's Hand Is in the Storm

That brings us to our second truth. It springs directly from the first, and both are the conclusions of faith.

In contrast to the cynicism of Joel's contemporaries who were driven to a hard-bitten agnosticism by the dreadful onslaughts of nature, and in contrast to the priests who found their faith crumbling before the savage visage of nature, Joel proposes another explanation both daring and comforting. If you have any poetry in your soul at all, read chapter 2 when you have a private moment. In a dramatic innovation, Joel sees the locusts descending out of the north as an army of the Lord. They come rank upon rank, company by company, devouring and destroying as they come. Walls do not stop them; they simply eat their way through them. Houses do not stop them; they simply march up and over them. Well disciplined, they tramp through the land, leaving it barren and desolate.

Joel contends they march at the command of the Lord!

Here is an insight we must not miss. Joel saw that this natural disaster was the hand of the Lord. God had not abandoned Judah. Nor had God forgotten Judah. Rather, God was deeply concerned and irrevocably committed to Judah and Jerusalem. The fierce countenance of nature was the evidence. The disaster was not evidence they were orphaned in the universe; it was proof they were God's very own.

Charles Beard, the great historian, says that one of the four lessons of history is that when it is dark enough you can see the stars. Joel's word to us who face the darkness of an unknown future is that God's stars glimmer in the darkness for those who look with eyes of faith.

George Truett, great-hearted preacher of the past generation, tells this true story out of his own pastoral experience.

I am thinking now of a strong man in yonder city, whose beautiful wife was taken from him after an illness of just a few hours, and the man was left with a little flaxen-haired girl, of some four or five summers. The body was carried out to the cemetery, where there was a simple service, and every heart was broken, the grief was so appalling. And then when the service was over, neighbors gathered around this big man and said to him: "You must come, with this little baby girl, and stay with us for several days. You must not go back to that home now." And the broken-hearted man said, "Yes, I must go right back to the same place where she was, . . . and I must fight it out with this baby right there," and back they went. He told about it all the next day. . . . Long and late the little one, in the crib there by the bed, sobbed, because she could not go to sleep, and the big man reached his hand over to the crib and petted her and mothered her, as best he could, and after awhile the little girl, out of sorrow for her father, stopped her crying—just out of sorrow for him. And in the darkness of that quiet time the big man looked through the darkness to God, and said, "I trust you, but, oh, it is as dark as midnight." And then the little girl started up her sobbing again, . . . And she said, "Papa, did you ever know it to be so dark? Why papa, I cannot even see you, it is so dark." And then, sobbing, the little thing said, "But, papa, you love me, if it is dark, don't you? You love me if I don't see you, don't you papa?" You know what he did. He reached across with those big hands and took the little girl out of her crib, and brought her over on his big heart, and mothered her, until at last, sobbing, the little thing fell to sleep, and then when she was asleep, he took his baby's cry to him, and passed it up to God, and said, "Father, it is as dark as midnight. I cannot see at all. But you love me, if it is dark, don't you?" . . . And then the darkness was like unto the morning! God always comes to people who trust Him.[3]

That was Joel's breathtaking contention. The storm was not an occasion for bitterness and cynicism. It was God's way of breaking up fallow ground.

God's Grace Covers Our Sin

We move then, with the irresistible logic of the prophet, to his conclusion. Since God's eye is on the sparrow and God's hand is in the storm, there is hope. This is the way the prophet expressed that hope: "Rend your heart, and not your garments, . . . And I will restore to you the years that the locust hath eaten" (2:13, 25).

Here is a word for all those broken resolutions, all those bright promises now tarnished and stained, all the hoped-for perfections never quite attained. Perhaps life has been closing in on you, and God seems distant and remote. There are years in your life that the locusts have eaten, and you now taste the wormwood and the gall. Or perhaps even now you can see the locusts descending, and you know why.

In the face of the locusts, Joel called for repentance. Only by repentance could Judah see God in the locusts. But should Judah repent, the scourge would be lifted, and the Lord God would restore all the years the locusts had eaten.

The way will not come any clearer for you until you honestly, wholeheartedly, even painfully, repent. This means not only to be sorry for the mess you have made of your life, but to surrender that mess and the life that created it to the Lord. It means to invite the Lord Christ into that inner citadel of your heart, where your values are determined and your judgments made, asking him to take over. To repent means to surrender.

The good tidings which Joel hinted at and the gospel which the apostles preached is this: when you make that surrender, God gives you of his own Spirit, so that you go forth clothed in God's strength. You do not see a miracle; you are a miracle. And God himself restores to you all that the locusts of those lost years have eaten.

Notes

1. R. Benjamin West, *Light Beyond Shadows* (New York: The Macmillan Company, 1959), p. 9.

2. Elizabeth Cheney, "Overheard in an Orchard," *Masterpieces* . . ., p. 86.

3. George W. Truett, *A Quest for Souls*, ed. J. B. Cranfill (Dallas, Texas: Baptist Standard Publishing Company, 1917), pp. 24-26.

11

The Potter and the Preacher

Jeremiah 18:1-6

The parable of the potter shop may provide an answer, or at least point a direction, for a very troublesome question. The question might be put something like this: how does God speak? If he were to speak to me, how would I know it? Would I hear an actual voice as Saul did? Or Isaiah? Or Moses?

George Bernard Shaw, in one of his plays, has a priest go into the cathedral before the altar and fairly shout into that heavy silence the demand of his questing heart: "God, speak to me!" According to Shaw, God did speak. The next morning, one of the sextons found the priest prostrate on the damp, stone floor, arms akimbo, cold in death. The voice of God was too much. Is it different with us?

So often we think of these men of the Bible and (I suspect) the preachers of our own day as having some special, unique faculty which enables them to hear what others may not hear, to know what others do not know, to possess a knowledge the average man in the pew cannot have. It is a kind of mystical "second sight" that some preachers claim.

But if God speaks straight out to preachers, then I must make a confession; I have never heard him. Not that way. I have as much difficulty knowing what God would have me do, of untangling my own inclinations and desires from God's will for me, as anybody I know. The only comfort I take is that I do not know many preachers to whom God *has* spoken aloud, either. This may be a deficiency in us, but if it is we can take comfort in the common affliction.

All of us have had the experience of having a hard decision to make, of weighing all the evidence pro and con, of measuring preference or ease, and then of making that hard decision. But there was no voice calling, no hand beckoning. Again, many of us have had an experience when the presence of God was very real and we were very sure, but even then there was nothing to touch, nothing anyone could have recorded on a tape or a film. For us that was a burning bush, but the rest were sitting around plucking blackberries.

So we are confronted in this passage by a common problem of human faith: how does God speak to us?

Jeremiah in perfect candor tells us how he "heard" this word of the Lord. He tells it without dissimulation or fancy footwork. He is plain and clear. In essence, the details are these: one day while out for a walk he happened by a potter shop. He stopped to watch, preoccupied. While the top of his mind was observing the potter at his work, the bottom of his mind was turning over a problem of the utmost gravity. It concerned the character of God.

Jeremiah was an astute observer of the times. He had risked his own personal safety to warn that the nation was fast drifting toward disaster. He had used all kinds of dramatic devices to make his sense of impending doom clear. He had taken some of his underclothing all the way over to the Euphrates in Babylon, left it there in a rock, and then later made a return trip to retrieve it. This was to symbolize the captivity. He had filled vessels with choicest wine, and then broken the vessels only to let the wine splatter out on the ground. This pictured the fate of Jerusalem's kings and princes. In the Valley of Hinnom Jeremiah had summoned the priests and community leaders, there to break treasured urns and vessels as a dramatic symbol of the broken treasures of Jerusalem.

But while Jeremiah was very sure of the imminent collapse of his beloved Jerusalem, he was not so sure of the morality of a God who would permit a blatant, arrogant heathenism to overrun this people of the covenant. True, Judah had sinned. She had broken the covenant. But Judah with all her sin was worlds better than heathen Babylon who made no pretense toward faith or morality at all.

In short, Jeremiah wondered at the ways of God.

Have you ever done that? Has it ever fallen on you to see a beloved friend stricken helpless by cancer? Or to see a modern Job stagger from one terrible stroke of fate to one even more terrible? Has the dark, nagging question of God's seemingly callous caprice ever really haunted you? Then you know the burden of Jeremiah that day in the potter's shop.

While Jeremiah watched the potter at work, suddenly he "heard the word of the Lord." That may be an awkward phrase for us. It was not so much what Jeremiah *heard* as what he *saw*. For as he watched the potter at work, Jeremiah *saw* a new truth; he caught glimpses of a new insight he had never seen before. What did he see?

Jeremiah observed the potter take his clay and mold a vessel. The vessel was defective, so he remolded it. Another did not work out as the potter originally intended it, so he adapted it to a modified form. Thought Jeremiah, "Is this not how God deals with Jerusalem?"

In that moment God communicated with his prophet, and the prophet could speak his new truth in a way that we today can understand it.

What was the word of the Lord that day to Jeremiah?

Inescapable Relatedness

As Jeremiah watched the potter at work with his clay, one of the earliest thoughts to come was that the clay and the potter were vitally interrelated. The potter was not entire without the clay; the clay was only clay without the potter. Each needed the other.

It is easy for us to imagine that we can do very well without the Father. Particularly is this true in our air-conditioned, push-button age. Content, insured, possessed of a sometime security, we fall under the illusion that we can make it very well on our own. In these moments of self-sufficiency we comfort ourselves with the thought that if worse comes to worst, the family will be taken care of by a combination of insurance, social security, and good luck. But the thought we cannot bear to face is this: what of us? What about this one, personal, indestructible cell of life called *me*? What happens to *me* when I am beyond the reach of money or medicine?

This question drives us back to an admission the Bible makes without any embarrassment at all, namely that the *me* all of us is concerned with would be nothing but a lump of clay without the Heavenly Father. Beautifully the Bible says: "And the Lord God formed man of the dust of the ground, and breathed into his nostrils the breath of life; and man became a living soul" (Gen. 2:7).

Now we can deny this truth; we can run from it; we can ignore it. But all the while it is there, staring us in the face. Sooner or later we must come to grips with it: there is no escaping our relatedness to the Father. The psalmist describes the inescapableness of our relatedness to the Father with a passage that many of us remember:

Thou compassest my path and my lying down, and art acquainted with all my ways. For there is not a word in my tongue, but, lo, O

Lord, thou knowest it altogether. Thou has beset me behind and
before, and laid thine hand upon me. Such knowledge is too wonderful for me; it is high, I cannot attain unto it. Whither shall I go from
thy spirit? or whither shall I flee from thy presence? If I ascend up
into heaven, thou art there: if I make my bed in hell, behold, thou
art there. If I take the wings of the morning, and dwell in the utter-
most parts of the sea; even there shall thy hand lead me, and thy
right hand shall hold me. If I say, Surely the darkness shall cover me;
even the night shall be light about me. Yea, the darkness hideth not
from thee . . . (Psalm 139:3-12).

Perhaps our trouble is that we know this to be true, but cannot
afford to admit it. The dilemma of our restless, driven, neurotic
age is the dilemma of a bad conscience. We are vitally related,
inescapably related, totally related to the Father, even as the
clay is related to the potter. But we may never really know this
until we have nothing left but the Father. Only then are we
aware that to have the Father is to have enough.

The Father's Freedom

The second part of this word of the Lord came a little slower.
Jeremiah had to watch the potter work awhile, and even then
the dawn came gradually. But eventually Jeremiah saw that the
potter was not bound in his art; he could improvise as he went.
If one form would not take shape, never mind; he could make
another.

Then Jeremiah saw this fact in relation to Judah. The Master
Potter was not bound by Judah and her Temple with its sacrifices and ritual. In fact, God had a kind of sovereign indifference
toward the whole business, as Jeremiah had come to see
(cf 7:21-23).

What God wanted was obedience; he wanted the sacrifice of
the heart (Psalm 40:6-8). And unless this is the form our faith
takes, he will pass it by! Only a consummate conceit would dare

think that our forms and our procedures are the only ones God can use. God is not bound to us, nor to what may be congenial to us. He is as free as a potter at his wheel. What God looks for is not form; it is function. He may want to fashion a new form.

Now what does all this have to do with me? you ask. I would answer quite simply that if any of us would have the fullest possible kind of life we must concede our relationship of dependency and then ask, "What wouldst thou have me to do?"

Clarence Tompkins, an ordinary Methodist preacher with an extraordinary compassion for old people, saw the need almost a generation ago for providing a place where men and women might spend the sunset years of life in comfort and earthly security. For more than a decade he fostered this dream in his Methodist conference. At last the conference passed a resolution approving it, and the bishop asked Dr. Tompkins to assume the challenge of putting flesh on bare bones.

It was a formidable task. Armed only with the good will of the conference and a pat on the back from his bishop, he went to work. Money was raised from the churches, but not enough. The whole project came to crisis. It was turn back or make the bold move. Tompkins made the bold move even while his bishop urged caution. With nothing but his own nerve and faith in God, the preacher promised an out-of-state financial institution repayment of a quarter of a million dollar loan in ten years, and on that promise received the additional funds necessary to begin.

Out on the flat prairie the first building of this fabulous institution rose up from the ground. In four years, that quarter of a million was repaid and $400,000 more had been raised and spent— almost a million dollars in five years to begin an institution that now has a budget of more than a million dollars a year, is worth in the millions, and is still expanding.

As I sat by this man who had dared to ask that question, "What wouldst thou have me to do?" a quarter of a century ago,

I noticed that his hands trembled so that he had to use both of them to pick up his cup of coffee. I said, "Men of your breed are rare, Doctor Tompkins. Not many of us are willing to pay the price." For the first time there was some registration of emotion as he said, "I never pass a simple village church, or an orphanage, or a school, but what I don't want to stop and take my hat off to salute the man through whom God did something different and unusual. And I want to salute the man because he was willing to pay the price. There is always a price."

> The world stands out on either side
> No wider than the heart is wide;
> Above the world is stretched the sky,—
> No higher than the soul is high.
> The heart can push the sea and land
> Farther away on either hand;
> The soul can split the sky in two,
> And let the face of God shine through.
> But East and West will pinch the heart
> That can not keep them pushed apart;
> And he whose soul is flat—the sky
> Will cave in on him by and by.
> EDNA ST. VINCENT MILLAY, "Renascence"

God is utterly free, and in his freedom he uses the vessels at his disposal.

The Father's Patience

The impassive patience of the potter of Hinnom spoke to Jeremiah of the patience of the Lord. But from here on the parable of the potter is not altogether true. For clay is *impersonal;* it has no will of its own. Any gap between design and product is a deficiency finally of the potter. So here we must take leave of Jeremiah and his rustic potter shop. Although he had truth, he did not have it all. It takes more than patience to make us pliable to the Master Potter; it takes conversion. For *we are personal;* we do have wills of our own; we can wreck the magnificent, wondrous design of the Father. And I should add, not only can, but do.

As we step outside the shop, we see a wondrous shadow cast upon it. It has the form of a cross. We turn from the shadow to face the cross itself. Can it be? Is the Potter also the crucified? What strange business is this? Here is a patience that no potter ever had. Here is an impliability that no potter ever found in his clay. What is it that will gently soften this hardness? It is not a threat; it is not harshness. If anything can reach through the hardness and make it pliable it is this strange sign, the cross, and what it signifies.

Then we remember a line from the New Testament that tells us just how infinite is the patience of the Master Potter: "God was in Christ, reconciling the world unto himself, not imputing their trespasses unto them; ... For he hath made him to be sin for us, who knew no sin; that we might be made the righteousness of God in him" (2 Cor. 5:19, 21).

If that wondrous truth cannot reach us, nothing can. There is nothing left except the judgment the Master Potter reserves for those who rebel to the very end.

12

The Watchman

Ezekiel 24:25-27; 33:7-11

In the earliest dawn of human history Cain asked the question: "Am I my brother's keeper?" We all feel an instinct to mouth the question of Cain, an altogether human instinct. The question strikes at the very heart of our responsibility for our neighbor. Jesus answered it in the parable of the good Samaritan, striking a blow at the priest and the Levite (and the modern man) who "pass by on the other side."

In his writings the prophet Ezekiel tells how he struggled with this all-too-human impulse. You will recall the essential details of his life. He had the misfortune and deprivation of being a refugee. Exiled to Babylon by Nebuchadnezzar in 597 B.C., he experienced the same paralysis of interest, the same dispirited outlook that seized all the banished.

Descending into a narrowing spiral of dejected self-pity, Ezekiel was prodded into larger concerns only by God's command that he be a watchman for the city, keeping his lonely vigil in the watchtower. For Ezekiel it was a mandate, and he shook off his lethargy to exercise a brave but unrewarding ministry for a period of nine years.

Suddenly a stroke of unkind fate took Ezekiel's wife. He describes that troubling event with severe economy: "I spake

90

unto the people in the morning: and at even my wife died; and I did in the morning as I was commanded" (24:18). So deep was the hurt of Ezekiel that he sank into a kind of speechless stupor that continued for two years. His earlier efforts had been met for the most part by an insufferable indifference or a condescending tolerance. Somehow, the price asked did not correspond to the value received. With a shrug of his shoulders and a sag in his posture, Ezekiel sank back into the miasma of self-pity.

It was two years later that an escaped refugee turned up in the camp near Babylon to report, "The city is smitten." It was the report of the fall of Jerusalem. The runner had taken six months for his journey. His looks corresponded to his tidings, and the sheer desperation of his mission, of his message, stabbed Ezekiel back into action. The old, familiar thought of the watchman came again to haunt him:

Son of man, I have set thee a watchman unto the house of Israel; therefore thou shalt hear the word at my mouth, and warn them for me. When I say unto the wicked, O wicked man, thou shalt surely die; if thou dost not speak to warn the wicked from his way, that wicked man shall die in his iniquity; but his blood will I require at thine hand. Nevertheless, if thou warn the wicked of his way to turn from it; if he do not turn from his way, he shall die in his iniquity; but thou hast delivered thy soul (33:7-9).

Ezekiel could not ignore, he could not be indifferent to the plight of his neighbor.

> There is a destiny that makes us brothers;
> None goes his way alone:
> All that we send into the lives of others
> Comes back into our own.[1]

This experience of Ezekiel speaks to a modern mood—this mood of impenetrable indifference. The magazine writer deals with the manifestation of this mood on a social level; here, we deal with this mood on a spiritual level. We may shrug it off, display a kind of sovereign indifference, ignore a smoldering and haunting sense of guilt. This impulse to mind our own business is strong, but it runs counter to the very heart of the biblical mission thrust. But Ezekiel, in complete candor, makes us face our desperate struggle to keep from getting involved.

The word which came to Ezekiel centered in the familiar figure of a watchman. That may not mean much to us; it did to Ezekiel. In your imagination picture a walled city. The only instruments of war are crude, limited in fire power and destructive capabilities. There are no planes and no rockets. Surprise is the deadliest foe. It is the watchman's business, day and night, to be alert for any sign of an approaching enemy. When he sees such, he is to give the warning upon which depends the safety and lives of all the residents of the city.

Spiritually, men and women are in constant danger of surprise attack by the dread enemy of their souls, the old adversary, the devil. The Father has set his own as watchmen in the night. The Father has done this because he takes no pleasure in the death of the wicked. That is Ezekiel's message to us.

Under Attack

The New Testament declares that it is not the possibility of attack that should alert us; it is the fact of a siege already underway: "For we wrestle not against flesh and blood, but against principalities, against powers, against the rulers of the darkness of this world, against spiritual wickedness in high places" (Eph. 6:12).

Take a familiar situation which we sometimes sum up with the phrase "keeping up with the Joneses." The family next door lives in the same income bracket, but they live more lavishly. Perhaps if we used our tithe carefully, we could piece out the higher payments for a new home and maybe throw in the additional cost of driving a new Cadillac. This is all very pleasing to the eye (and the ego), and the devil has us, like Eve, off balance. Unless we resort to our spiritual armor and prayer, it is only a matter of time until the devil will administer the *coup de grace*.

Or consider the instinct to be the free, unrestrained, undisciplined prodigal out in the far country. Who has not known that instinct? If we were to be completely honest, we would have to admit to a secret, troublesome envy of that prodigal who takes Sunday for his own, who lives by his own code, who has cut all the attached strings. Oh, it is not there all of the time; it just crops out now and then making us feel crochety, imposed on, touchy. Sometimes, our dose of religion is just enough to make us miserable, not enough to make us free and happy. We can only conclude that while an angel may have us by the hand, the devil often has us by the heart.

Dostoevski, who was himself both angel and devil, has a passage in his works which describes this ambivalence we have all known in greater or lesser degree:

I got to the point of feeling a sort of secret abnormal despicable enjoyment in returning home to my corner on some disgusting Petersburg night, acutely conscious that that day I had committed a loathsome action again, that what was done could never be undone, and secretly, inwardly gnawing, gnawing at myself for it, tearing and consuming myself.[2]

The Watchman

This inner wretchedness may go unrecognized for what it is without someone to trace it out for us. That someone is the watchman.

In Ezekiel, the watchman is the prophet himself. The entire parable focuses upon him and his function. He has fallen into idleness. The word comes to quicken him, to stab him into action. As we read this eternal word coming to Ezekiel, it suddenly becomes contemporary, leaps off the page, and confronts us with our own responsibility to our own age. As in Ezekiel's age, so now. The question is being asked, indirectly often, but with a pathetic insistence: "Watchman, what of the night?"

This is a question we would like to avoid, and for various reasons. For one thing it is *more comfortable* to be silent. We hesitate to bear the brand "fanatic." It just isn't that important, we think. After all, spiritual realities are deeply personal, and who am I to go prying around in this intimate area of somebody else's history? They are adult; they know what they want; I'll leave them alone.

There's only one trouble with that. The very fact that we meet resistance tells us that here is an unmet need so deep that this acquaintance, this loved one, this friend, is unwilling to face it. Am I a friend—a watchman—if I blithely ignore what is as plain as day?

Joseph Conrad pictures the grey kind of damnation that falls on men and women because they are unwilling to face hard, somber, and foreboding facts. Conrad's novel *Typhoon* concerns Captain MacWhirr, who is sailing a cargo of two hundred Chinese coolies back to their native village after a few years of work in tropical colonies. En route, the ship is caught in the throes of a typhoon, and the havoc that follows can only be laid at the door of the captain who refused to believe the signs the sea gave before the storm struck. Conrad, in an unusual paragraph, describes the captain's insensible insensitivity:

The sea itself had never put itself out to startle the silent man, who seldom looked up, and wandered innocently over the waters with the only visible purpose of getting food, raiment, and houseroom for three people ashore. Dirty weather he had known, of course. He had been made wet, uncomfortable, tired in the usual way, felt at the time and presently forgotten. . . . But he had never been given a glimpse of immeasurable strength and of immoderate wrath, the wrath that passes exhausted but never appeased—the wrath and fury of the passionate sea. He knew it existed, as we know that crime and abominations exist; he had heard of it as a peaceable citizen in a tour hears of battles, famines, and floods, and yet knows nothing of what these things mean. . . . Captain MacWhirr had sailed over the surface of the oceans as some men go skimming over the years of existence to sink gently into a placid grave, ignorant to the last, without ever having been made to see all it may contain of perfidy, violence, and of terror. There are on sea and land such men.[3]

Conrad is speaking of the myriads of men and women who by their dullness and insensitivity wreak damnation and destruction in our world. They are watchmen who seek comfort through a dull silence.

Could I name one other reason why we are sometimes silent? We have an aversion to *involvement*. We just do not want to get our hands all messy, our affairs all complicated, our privacy invaded. Nobody gets more involved than a watchman. We prefer to be detached. So we hold our peace.

But there is a price attached to detachment. A good word for it would be guilt. I shall ever feel a sense of guilt over my failure to be a watchman to a dying woman on my paper route as a youthful teen-ager. I kept silent until the day the black crepe hung on the door, though I often sensed her weakness, and I often stifled the impulse to speak that word of concern.

Albert Camus tells a haunting story of an established, impeccable French lawyer who has had his world in complete control until the night he hears a drowning woman's cry as he passes along the Seine River. He merely turns away rather than be involved, and in so doing, mirrors many of us. Mirrored also is the guilt Camus' lawyer feels, a guilt that drives him, ruins him, and makes him cry out years later in remorse as he talks to himself in an Amsterdam bar: "O young woman, throw yourself into the water again so that I may a second time have the chance of saving both of us!"

Like Camus' lawyer, we cannot escape the fact that we are watchmen, and in a far more profound sense than he.

The Pleasure of the Lord

Clearly involved in Ezekiel's summons was the pleasure and purpose of the Lord God. The word came to the prophet explicitly: "I have no pleasure in the death of the wicked." Ezekiel was to persuade men of the goodness of God, of his yearning to forgive, of the aching void in the Father's heart.

Ezekiel did what he could the rest of his days, not because he liked to, but because he felt he had to. The only credential he had was himself, the only proof, his own inner certainty. He used his considerable powers of persuasion and won those who would believe. But his gospel was essentially a negative gospel, warning only of the judgment upon sin.

Our task is not quite so hard. We have an evidence Ezekiel did not have, the crucified, risen Saviour. We have a fellowship he could not offer, the fellowship of the redeemed. But one thing has not changed: the fact that we are watchmen because the Father has laid his hand upon us and made us partakers of his grace.

Some years ago a senior editor of *Time* magazine disclosed to the Congressional Committee on Un-American Activities that a trusted officer of the State Department had earlier been a fellow-member of the Communist conspiracy with him. To volunteer this information was a difficult decision, one that immediately exposed him to abuse and calumny of the worst possible kind. When the ordeal was finally over and Alger Hiss had been condemned and sentenced, Whittaker Chambers wrote a book of his experiences which he titled *Witness Whittaker Chambers*. In the introduction to that book, Mr. Chambers wrote these lines:

I do not know any way to explain why God's grace touches a man who seems unworthy of it. But neither do I know any other way to explain how a man like myself—tarnished by life, unprepossessing, not brave—could prevail so far against the powers of the world arrayed almost solidly against him to destroy him and defeat his truth. In this sense I am an involuntary witness to God's grace and to the fortifying power of faith.[4]

That is the sense in which we are watchmen, and any who are under this compulsion will not deny its power.

Notes

1. Markham, "A Creed," *Masterpieces* . . ., p. 464.
2. Theodore Dostoevski, "Notes from Underground," *The Short Novels of Dostoevski,* ed. Thomas Mann (New York: Dial Press, 1945), p. 132.
3. Joseph Conrad, "Typhoon," *Portable Conrad* (New York: Doubleday and Company, Inc., 1959), p. 207. Used by permission of J. M. Dent and Sons, Ltd., London.
4. Whittaker Chambers, *Witness Whittaker Chambers* (New York: Random House, 1952), p. 6.

13

Can These Bones Live?

Ezekiel 37:1-10

Once Ezekiel had stooped to pick up the burden of his thankless ministry again, he was faced with an agony that our comforts make unimaginable. Here was a people—the remnant of a once proud nation—without country, without home, without a future, and therefore without hope. For these exiles far from home, the news of the final surrender and sacking of Jerusalem snuffed out the last flickering candle of their lives. A proverb passed back and forth among them which faithfully reflected the darkness of their despair: "Our bones are dried; our hope is lost; we feel ourselves cut off."

Ezekiel could not forget that proverb: "Our bones are dried; our hope is lost; we feel ourselves cut off." It lay like sullen death upon his spirit; it weighed on his heart; it darkened his mental powers. "Our bones are dried; our hope is lost; we are cut off."

Ezekiel was no stranger to the deepest kind of depression, and often before he had found relief by walking alone out on the plains of Shinar. It was here he had first caught his vision of God riding omnipotent and splendid, giving direction to the affairs of men. Perhaps it was out here that he had recovered his tongue, after two long years of helpless, involuntary aphasia. It was out here that Ezekiel had his burden lifted, the candle of hope rekindled for himself and his nation. In an ecstatic seizure, Ezekiel felt and heard the word of the Lord.

The essential features of this experience are dramatic enough. In his ecstatic seizure, Ezekiel looks out over a valley upon a scene which he can scarcely take in. It is a grim, grisly scene, like something from a horror movie. As far as the eye can see in every direction, Ezekiel sees nothing but the blanched, dry, skeletal bones of men and women. It is a ghastly and graphic scene, pieced together from the passing proverb: "Our bones are dried; our hope is lost; we are cut off."

Even while Ezekiel seeks to comprehend the meaning of all this, a sepulchral voice cries out to him: "Son of man, can these bones live?" Ezekiel is too overwhelmed to answer, indeed, to think. He can only say, "Thou knowest, Lord."

Then the story takes a strange turn: the prophet is told to cry over these bleached, chalky bones a kind of mysterious incantation. He tells the story quite directly:

He said unto me, Prophesy upon these bones, and say unto them, O ye dry bones, hear the word of the Lord. Thus said the Lord God unto these bones; Behold, I will cause breath to enter into you, and ye shall live: And I will lay sinews upon you, and will bring flesh upon you, and cover you with skin, and put breath in you, and ye shall live; and ye shall know that I am the Lord (37:5-6).

The next scene would challenge the imagination of the most inventive of scenario directors. "So I prophesied as I was commanded: and as I prophesied, there was a noise, and behold a shaking, and the bones came together, bone to his bone (7:7). The old Negro spiritual, with its graphic and detailed accounting of this event, gives us some idea of what Ezekiel saw:

The head bone connected to the neck bone; the neck bone connected to the chest bone; the chest bone connected to the back bone;

the back bone connected to the hip bone; the hip bone connected to
the leg bone; the leg bone connected to the shin bone; the shin bone
connected to the ankle bone; the ankle bone connected to the foot
bone—oh, hear the Word of the Lord!

And hear that word they did. But bones—even skeletons—are
not living, breathing, pulsating men. They are only dry bones.
The question remains: Can these bones live?

That question is not long in getting an answer. For in the next
moment, the prophet describes an unbelievable scene: sinew
and flesh and skin cover those bones! Now the valley lies strewn
with bodies. But they are dead bodies; there is no life in them.

Once again the word of the Lord comes:

Prophesy unto the wind, prophesy, son of man, and say to the wind,
Thus said the Lord God; Come from the four winds, O breath, and
breathe upon these slain, that they may live. So I prophesied as he
commanded me, and the breath came into them, and they lived, and
stood up upon their feet, an exceeding great army (37:9-10).

When we look at the chapter in its entirety, we find that
Ezekiel had nothing to hide. The point of this whole vision he
makes quite clear: now that Israel's past was smashed, she could
move into a new future with a boldness and stature that could
only emerge out of the ashes of her past. The proverb was right
in its description of the events of history so far; the proverb
was wrong in the conclusion drawn. This was not the end of
life; it was the beginning. The dead bones of Israel would revive.

There is an instinct in us to brush aside this bizarre, ecstatic
trance as a relic of an outgrown age—interesting, even exciting,
but wholly irrelevant. Yet, there is in us a growing suspicion that
in the passing forms of this bedouin dreamer are abiding truths.
Does this vision of the valley of dry bones have anything to say
to us today?

Certainly, couched in the transient drama of Ezekiel and his nation is the eternal word of God, vital for us in our day even as it was vital for the exiles of that bygone day in Babylon.

When you examine the broad movement of the vision, it seems to fall quite naturally into four parts. The drama begins with the vision of death: a valley filled with bleached, dry bones. The next scene is the most enigmatic, apparently the most futile: the prophet, preaching over dead bones, and this strange, other-worldly phenomenon, the stirring and the joining of the bones. Then comes scene three, with the wind gently passing over these dead bodies. Scene four completes the drama. These bodies have revived; for death there is life; the dead bones live!

Is this not a condensed analysis and a hopeful promise both for the broken person and our broken world? Let us see.

The Vision of Death

In 1947 a French Swiss medical doctor and psychiatrist wrote a book entitled *The Whole Person in a Broken World*. Seventeen years later this book was translated into English and published here in America. The book is so contemporary to our 1966 that the only revision necessary after this lapse of more than a decade and a half was a total of about two and a half pages.

The significance of that is simply this: the march of civilization—the technological progress that has taken place since World War II—has not essentially changed the spiritual and moral dilemma of our world. If anything, we are sicker now than fifteen years ago. This is what the doctor has to say about the desperate malady central to most of our lives:

The typical sickness of our epoch is neurosis. Many doctors agree that more than half of their patients suffer from it. And this is not accidental. The cause of it is that our materialistic and amoral civilization no longer answers the deepest needs of the soul.

Pavlov's experiments upon animals have shown that neurosis is tied up with a kind of spiritual irresolution, or as the psychologists express it, with an ambivalence. The modern soul is hesitant. . . . The world tells him that feeling, faith, and philosophical truth are unimportant. And this same man cherishes at the bottom of his heart a justified intuition that these problems are nevertheless important. His thirst for love, his spiritual loneliness, his fear of death, the riddle of evil, the mystery of God—he no longer speaks of these things; he represses them, but still they haunt him.

There is "an inner conflict between a false suggestion and a true intuition. A false suggestion from the modern world and a true intuition of the soul, which in reality yearns for something altogether different from science, power, and material goods."[1]

But the doctor is only describing clinically the symptoms of a New Testament diagnosis. For the New Testament has put our inner world under the microscope, and come up with a startling conclusion: "You are dead in your trespasses and your sins." There comes upon us a suspicion that perhaps Ezekiel saw to the very heart of things when he peered out across a valley strewn with death; and when we consult our own inner disquiet, we know that the broken world around us is only a faithful reflection of our own broken, fragmented, torn lives. Indeed, the only thing that can surpass our guilt would be God's grace. This is a fact no sinner of us would deny. If we deny it, we only bare our own spiritual malaise.

The Task of the Preacher

Ezekiel, you will remember, was commanded to preach in that valley of death. Could there be anything more futile?

Of course, we read the story with the advantage of knowing the final scene. But for the moment, let us cancel out that knowledge. What we have left closely corresponds with our own present situation: a desperate sense of tornness, of guilt, and a preacher preaching. Will it do any good?

Sometimes preachers are haunted by a sense of futility. Week after week, year after year, we preach. But nothing much changes. The old earth takes another spin or two; men choose up sides on first one question and then another; violence and destruction break out; and death finally comes to silence the restless hearts of men who agitated both sides of the question.

Can preaching change anything?

This question goes deeper than the mere mechanics of preaching, although that also has its vital relevance, as pastor Fred E. Luchs of the First Congregational Church of Ann Arbor, Michigan, can testify. He was questioning his little daughter about Bible personalities:

> "Who was Matthew?"
> "I don't know, but I know who Stephen was."
> "Who was he?"
> "A preacher."
> "What happened to him?"
> "He was stoned to death."
> "Why?"
> "Because his sermons weren't any good."

But beyond the mechanics of the sermon and the style of the preacher is this matter of preaching itself. Is it an exercise in futility?

Preaching God's message has always been open to ridicule and misunderstanding. Ezekiel tells us, in a moment of rare self-disclosure, of the contradiction posed by his own personal popularity with the people and the seeming indifferent response they made to his message (33:30-33). Paul struggled with this same question and concluded that preaching, like the death of Jesus on the cross, involved the mystery of God's power coming to men in the guise of weakness (1 Cor. 1:18-29). But it has been the modern behaviorist psychologists who have left us clues that show the wisdom of God in the foolishness of preaching. Pavlov, the Russian scientist, who conditioned dogs to salivate at the mere sound of a bell, concluded: "Words are more important to men than reality." The diabolical cunning of propaganda— whether from the East or the West, as well as the assumption of all modern radio and TV advertising—rests squarely on this fact: words do change men. Words reach into the inner world, where men compare, decide, and will. The reality remains unchanged. How men see that reality, however, depends upon their vantage point. Words, and ideas that come by words, change the vantage point, and because preaching involves words, preaching is important.

But what of the message? Beyond the fact of preaching is the message the preacher proclaims. What is that message? For the Christian preacher it is essentially centered in history, a thing which God has done in the midst of men, a mysterious yet open disclosure of the very heart of the Heavenly Father in the life, death, resurrection, and abiding presence of Jesus Christ in the lives of his own. Words can never fully explain this great thing the Father has done, but we must employ our poor words in our best effort.

When this message is proclaimed in its fulness, transformations do take place.

Some time ago a writer in the *Sunday School Times* told of John Richard Green who, with a burning passion to help his fellowmen, went from the university down to the wretchedness and sin of East London. He established libraries, taught classes, cleaned streets, improved homes, fed the hungry. But after ten years, he said: "It's no use. They will go on drinking and gambling to the end." He left it all and went back to Oxford to write the history of England.

But down into that same section of the city came William Booth and his wife Catherine. They had nothing to offer except the message of what God had done for all men in Jesus. They preached that message and lived lives of sacrificial service in the name of him whom they preached. What John Green with his wealth and humanitarian impulses could not do, William Booth did: he changed East London. How? Under the preaching of the gospel of Jesus Christ, thousands were transformed and made to become the children of God.

That is part of the task of the preacher.

The Preacher Is the Sermon

But his task involves more than the craft of putting words together; it involves the preacher himself. More than any preacher is willing to admit, his preaching is confessional. What the preacher is, his preaching will disclose.

That makes every sermon something more than a "put-up job." What Robert Frost once said about a poem might also be said about a sermon: "A poem is never a put-up job, so to speak. It begins as a lump in the throat, a sense of wrong, a homesickness, a lovesickness. It is never a thought to begin with."[2] A sermon has something of the sermonizer in it. Robert Murray McCheyne preached in Dundee, Scotland, until at age thirty, he died. A young preacher visiting that church asked the sexton, "How did he prepare his sermons that so melted and moved the people to God?" The sexton showed him the famous preacher's chair. "Sit down there," he said, "and put your head in your hands. Now, let the tears flow. That's how he did it." J. Wallace Hamilton, who tells the story, remarks, "That is how every great evangel did it." But preaching is not in the past tense. If preaching is to make any difference now, it must be the same. The preacher must throw his heart over the pulpit first, then let his words follow. If the preacher be faithful to the heart of the Heavenly Father, then some will hear unto repentance and new life.

The Quickening Spirit

Ezekiel preached, and there was this strange stirring across the valley. But the end result was form without life: "There was no breath in them."

Could that be a description of modern Christianity?

The New Testament speaks of a kind of Christianity that "has a form of godliness, but denies the power thereof" (2 Tim. 3:5). The word translated "power" here is used often in the New Testament to express the means by which God discloses himself to men through Christ: a power that is turned inside out, that has the appearance of weakness, that belies first impressions. So the gospel is called "the power of God" (Rom. 1:16); and Jesus is called the "power of God" (1 Cor. 1:24).

But this derivative Christianity does not have that kind of power. It is impressive at first, but will not bear inspection. To use Ezekiel's term, "there is no breath" there. It cannot deliver in the long haul.[3]

Isn't that the kind of Christianity that is all too real? A kind of sham piety, with no vital, dynamic power? Anyone who is acquainted with modern church life, who has seen it from the inside, will readily recognize a prevailing condition. Whole classes of grown, adult people do not have enough inner, spiritual drive to break the chains of their own fatalistic, introspective, self-preoccupation. Groups of adults feed on their teachers and leaders, want everything done for them and want to do nothing themselves, are experts at ticking off hypochondriacal symptoms of a deep-seated anxiety, and are almost cannibalistic in their drain on those who would try to help. Like a drowning man fights his would-be rescuer, so these modern church members squeeze the life out of those who try to meet their insatiable thirst for ministry and attention.

Sometimes we talk about a "winning witness." But there is

nothing "winning" about that kind of witness. It is the best recommendation against itself I know. What is wrong? Why all these evidences of a deep, inner unsoundness of spirit? Could it be the complete absence of the Holy Spirit? "Where the Spirit of the Lord is, there is liberty" (2 Cor. 3:17). There are areas of modern church life where we need to have a breath of fresh air pass through.

It was this figure of the wind passing through by which Ezekiel captured the idea of the necessity of the Spirit. Perhaps he said more than he knew, but for us it is axiomatic: without the Spirit of God in our midst, we have nothing but form and motion. Like the Negro deacon, we may be a little hard-pressed to put the reality of the Spirit in words, but we can detect his absence. The deacon complained that his preacher did not "preach in the Spirit." Asked what he meant by that, the good man could only reply, "I don't know just how to say what it is, but I sure does know when it ain't."

In a more refined way, Christina Rossetti speaks of the same reality:

> Who has seen the wind?
>   Neither I nor you;
> But when the leaves hang trembling,
>   We know the wind is passing through.
>
> Who has seen the wind?
>   Neither you nor I;
> But when the trees bow down their heads
>   We know the wind is passing by.[4]

But lest we be misled, we must understand that the Spirit, like the wind, can only pass through openings, not closures. Even in a worship service there is a dual responsibility. The minister's responsibility we have seen, at least in part; but what of the pew? To be spiritually prepared to *hear* a sermon involves some definite responsibility. I am not sure this list is exhaustive, but it is suggestive:

First, be present. No sermon will help if you are not present to hear it.

Second, be prayerful. Pray for yourself, for the congregation gathering, for the choir, the musicians, the preacher. Such prayer will draw the best from you and all the others who share the hour of worship with you.

Third, become involved. This would mean participate in singing, in praying, in giving. Worship at bottom is self-giving. It must be wholehearted if it be worthy.

Fourth, be receptive. It is easy for us—and we must be on our guard here—to shut out another because of some unconscious rejection, some unrecognized hostility. I recall preaching in a revival in a great Midwestern city where, after an evening service, a visitor came to me with a confession. "When you stood up to preach," he said, "I thought immediately of . . ." (and he named a prominent TV entertainer whom he thought I resembled). "But I lifted a little prayer that the Spirit would remove that block, and he did. I want to thank you for the blessing I received from your sermon tonight." Be receptive.

Finally, be a doer. "Be ye doers of the word, and not hearers only," said James (1:22). Kierkegaard reminds us: "The highest of all is not to understand the highest but to act upon it."[5] The New Testament makes action under the impression of the Holy Spirit the touchstone of our Christianity. "For as many as are led by the Spirit of God, they are the sons of God" (Rom. 8:14).

That is a hard saying, but no harder than the truly Christian way is narrow. We need more of the Spirit in our lives, with his power transforming our weakness into strength. We ought to pray as the poet prayed.

Come, Holy Spirit, heav'nly Dove,
With all Thy quick'ning pow'rs;
Kindle a flame of sacred love
In these cold hearts of ours.

In vain we tune our formal songs;
In vain we strive to rise;
Hosannas languish on our tongues,
And our devotion dies.

Come, Holy Spirit, heav'nly Dove,
With all Thy quick'ning pow'rs;
Come, shed abroad the Savior's love,
And that shall kindle ours.

ISAAC WATTS

The Revival of Hope

Ezekiel proclaimed his message; the bones gathered to one another, adding sinew and flesh; the Spirit moved; and then the miracle: "The breath came into them, and they lived, and stood up upon their feet" (37:10). With the final eclipse of Jerusalem at hand that new life was intended to confirm hope for the prophet. But that passage can be read in the first person also, for in it are the essential elements of conversion.

Imagine my promising: "So you want to be an author? I can give you the spirit of Shakespeare." Think of the literary genius you might become!

Or you want to be a musician and composer? Suppose I could say, "I know how you may have the spirit of Mozart." What a musician you could be!

Or perhaps you would like to be a poet. I might say, "I know how you can have the spirit of Robert Frost." You would be thrilled and wondering at the possibilities.

Or it may be that you want to be an engineer. Imagine my saying, "I know how you can have the spirit of Kettering."

But that is impossible. There is no way I know by which you can possess the spirit of Shakespeare, Mozart, Frost, Kettering or any other blithe spirit which has blessed the human family—with one exception.

Suppose you want to be a better person. Imagine that I say to you, "I know how you can have the Spirit of Jesus." This is not beyond you. This is a possibility. The New Testament clearly states, "If any man be in Christ, he is a new ceature: old things are passed away; behold all things are become new" (2 Cor. 5:17). This promise I do offer, not because of what I can do but because of what Christ has already done.

Once, in the midst of a storm threatening to overturn his ship, a rough, cursing, self-willed sailor knelt and prayed for the first time in his life. Later on, John Newton was to call that experience his conversion, and he spent over forty years of his life thereafter preaching the gospel of Christ.

When he died, Newton had this epitaph put on a stone in the church he had served in London:

John Newton, Clerk

Once an Infidel and Libertine,
A servant of Slaves in Africa,
Was by the rich mercy of our
Lord and Saviour Jesus Christ,
Preserved, Restored and Pardoned,
And Appointed to Preach the Faith
He Had Long Laboured to Destroy.[6]

Notes

1. Paul Tournier, *The Whole Person in a Broken World* (New York: Harper & Row, 1964), pp. 11-12.

2. Louis Untermeyer, *Robert Frost, A Backward Look,* Library of Congress Reference Department pamphlet. L. C. Card 64-60031 [Washington, D.C., 1964], p. 23.

3. Cf. Alan Richardson, *The Miracle Stories of the Gospels* (London: Student Christian Movement Press, Ltd., 1963), cf. chapter 1.

4. Christina Rossetti, "The Wind," *Masterpieces* . . ., p. 1.

5. Soren Kierkegaard, *Journals,* ed. and trans. Alexander Dru (London: Collins Clear-Type Press, Fontana Books, 1958), p. 213.

6. Harvey B. Marks, *The Rise and Growth of English Hymnody* (New York: Fleming H. Revell Company, 1938), p. 110.

14

Zechariah's Lamp

Zechariah 4:1-4, 13-14

This chapter in Zechariah reads with an artful suspense faintly reminiscent of the delightful Arabian tales of Shaharazad. Moreover, the distinctly Oriental, almost bizarre figure of Zechariah's golden lampstand, topped with a golden bowl, reminds us of the story of Aladdin's lamp—with one difference.

Aladdin's lamp points to no particular moral truth; the story is told to entertain. Zechariah's lamp, however, exists to point up a spiritual truth underlying the whole of life; the story is told to edify. This is the difference.

The Twin Pillars

The essential details of the vision are these. In the center of the picture is the golden lampstand topped by a golden bowl, with seven candles distributed around its perimeter. These seven candles (or lamps) burn day and night without interruption and are identified in verse 10 as "the eyes of the Lord, which run to and fro through the whole earth." The lighted lamps would suggest the presence of the Lord in the midst of the people.

Beside the golden lampstand on either side is an olive tree. Leading from each tree to the lampstand is a pipe, and in this pipe flows the olive oil which keeps the lamps burning. The two trees are identified in verse 14 as "the two annointed ones" which can only be Joshua, the high priest, and Zerubbabel, the governor. These men, we surmise, are the centers of concern.

What is it Zechariah would say? Is it not that the twin pillars of any society—the institutions of government and religious faith —must nourish and sustain a personal sense of the presence of God in the midst of the people? that the church and the state must reinforce the acceptance and the practice of religious truth in the private life of the nation? that a society rests and depends upon theological belief? But there remains the thorny problem of mixing church with state. Can this be valid for us?

On the one side is the state. What responsibility does the state have to nurture theological belief? any at all? The secularists would declare that the state can only serve secular means, that any reference toward God in any function of state is ill-advised and inappropriate.

Now this might very well be contended were it not for the confounding fact that men administer the functions of the state; and men exercise an independent judgment. The law may be above theology (though I doubt it); the man who administers the law is not. His theological assumptions will determine how impartially and how fairly he functions. Without theological presuppositions, the officer on the beat and the judge on the bench each will have his eye on the highest dollar. When justice is determined by the highest bidder, there is no justice.

In the simple matter of a traffic ticket, theological belief can be involved. An exasperated salesman abandoned his car in a no-parking zone and left this note: "I've circled this block 20 times. I have an appointment and must keep it or lose my job. Forgive us our trespasses."

Now it is possible that the officer might have taken a more lenient attitude toward that infraction had a five dollar bill been pinned to the note. But, alas, it was not, and the officer left a ticket pinned to the note with this addition: "I've circled this block 20 years. If I don't give you a ticket I'll lose my job. Lead us not into temptation."

One of our recent major presidential candidates has driven with an unerring instinct to the heart of this matter in remarks he is reported to have made at the Illinois State Fair:

There is something distinctly wrong when common honesty and familiar morality are openly and widely challenged by the doctrine of the fast buck and the code of the off-color novel. There is something wrong when the standards of drama and literature seek new depths rather than new heights; when pornography becomes a measure of talent. . . .

There is a mood of easy morals and uneasy ethics that is an aching truth in our land. And no one in a position to set the examples that might set this right can avoid responsibility for what is wrong. Let me put it this way: there should be no skeletons in the closets of any part of the federal structure, and that goes for the smallest agency right up to the White House itself.[1]

On the other side of Zechariah's lampstand was the priest. He would represent for us the minister. Could it be possible that the church and her ministers fail to feed private faith? One of our seminary presidents intimates that it is not only possible; it is a fact of modern church life. Duke McCall, president of Southern Baptist seminary, Louisville, Kentucky, writing in a recent issue of that institution's *Tie* magazine, contends that much of our Southern Baptist preaching is no longer prophetic; it is liturgical. What he means, if I understand him, is that we are content to use old clichés, shibboleths, and a worn-out language of Zion that makes a good sound but says nothing. The congregation wants to be soothed; the preacher wants to be petted; the prophetic word—the live communication of God's truth for our day—is never uttered.[2]

That is a serious charge, and I do not take it altogether seriously. But in whatever measure it is true, in that measure the church and the minister of today are failing to fulfil the role Zechariah assigns to them. The minister must constantly address himself to two separate segments of his world. With one eye on the public scene, the church and her ministers must be God's plumb line; with the other eye on the private domain, the church and her ministers together must be the shepherd of the sheep. To neglect either segment of this dual responsibility is to fail in some measure to do the task given.

The man who functions in the life of the church and the man who functions in the life of the state each has his own peculiar responsibility as one of the twin pillars of society. This is the meaning of the olive trees on either side of the golden lampstand.

A Nation's Strength

Closely related to the idea of the twin pillars in Zechariah's lampstand is the idea of the nation's strength. It might be stated as an axiomatic corollary: a nation will be no stronger than its private faith. This is so obvious that we may miss it; but the truth abides. The strength of a nation is not in its rockets, missiles, or nuclear megaton bombs; its strength is in the character of its people.

I cannot help but wonder if the tragic life of Ira Hayes does not present in concentrated form the tragedy of modern America. Ira Hayes was one of the six men who raised a flag on Iwo Jima during World War II and one of three who survived that day of battle. He returned to America a celebrated war hero. His valor, his courage, his bravery were extolled by the nation. The scene itself has been immortalized in bronze.

But what of Hayes? He returned to his home in southern Arizona, and in spite of the efforts of friends and welfare groups to help him, he became a hopeless alcoholic. He was arrested fifty-one times for public drunkenness. At the age of thirty-two, he died of exposure and alcoholism. What the strength of the enemy outside could not accomplish the weakness of the enemy inside did. It was a sad ending for a national hero. I wonder if it might not presage the sad ending of a nation, invincible before their enemies, destroying themselves through a failure of self-discipline.

Veiled Power

We move on to our final thought, that of veiled power. Zechariah belonged to a deprived generation. Deprived, but brave. He was one of those who returned to the rubble of Jerusalem, now strewn over the top of Zion, barren in the desert sun. With the comforts of Babylon behind and the bleak prospects of the reconstructed Jerusalem before, Zechariah was compelled to mix a generous portion of faith with present reality in order that he not lose heart altogether. And Zechariah was one who could see the shape of the future in the grim facts of the present.

If you read the entire chapter, you will find two sentences Zechariah weaves into the story of his lamp, both of which hint at a veiled and unseen power. One of the sentences is this: "Not by might, nor by power, but by my spirit, saith the Lord" (v. 6). The other reads: "Who hath despised the day of small things?" (v. 10).

Right here Zechariah bared the divine method. It was the divine method for reclaiming Jerusalem; but even more, it is the divine method for reclaiming a lost man.

When our Father decided it was time, he came to men veiled in weakness—the weakness of a baby, crying in the stall of a barn. In the events that followed the birth of that baby, it was never suspected by most that this one life was the most momentous thing that had ever happened in the history of man. Only after his brave and untimely death on a cross, followed by resurrection, was it suspicioned that here was something more than an isolated event in Palestine; here was a cosmic event for all the world. For "God was in Christ, reconciling the world unto himself" (2 Cor. 5:19).

The apostle Paul calls this veiled power the wisdom of God (1 Cor. 1:21). It is so foreign to our own naked will to power, our driving will to be loved, our bare will to manipulate and dominate, that it requires the illumination of the Holy Spirit to understand just what it is God has done. But when we have eyes to see and understand, we discover that though Jesus came veiled in weakness, there was behind that veil a power that defeats evil. We meet it first in the record given us in the New Testament. It is not a claim made; it is a deed done. A deed done not once, but over and over again. As Professor Harnack has so beautifully explained it:

Jesus says very little about sickness; He cures it. He does not explain that sickness is health; He calls it by its proper name, and has compassion upon the sick person. There is nothing sentimental or artificial about Jesus; He draws no fine distinctions, and utters no sophistries.[3]

It is not what Jesus says; it is what he does. It is true in the New Testament; it is also true in our own experience. We are convinced by what Jesus does.

In a recent revival series, I went with the pastor to visit a family in the community. We found a lovely family: two teenagers, a smaller child, a mother and father. The evidences were abundant that they had no real physical needs. But there was a deep spiritual need. The father was addicted to strong drink; his addiction hung like a pall over the whole family. The pastor confided that the father had not come home the past Friday evening from work; he had been out from Friday until early Sunday, and when he came in, it was in pitiable condition. An invitation was extended to them to attend revival services.

The next evening, the mother and father were present with the family. The first to make a decision about her spiritual life was the mother. She was the only one of that family to respond that night. The week sped on to Saturday night, and that night this father and two teen-age sons made their move. What a difference that week had made!

The following day the revival came to a close. After the final service, the father took my hand, and with visible emotion said, "You'll never know what this revival and your preaching has meant to me. You helped me find my way again."

I thought about my preaching, and about 1 Corinthians 1. It was not my preaching that did it; it was the message preached.

Notes

1. Hedley Donavan, "The Difficulty of 'Being Fair' to Goldwater," *Life*, LVII (September 12, 1964), 104.

2. Duke K. McCall, "Thinking Aloud," *The Tie* (September, 1964), 2.

3. Adolph Von Harnack, *Expansion of Christianity*, trans. Thomas Bailey Saunders (3rd ed., New York: G. P. Putnam's Sons, 1901), p. 121.

15

The Power of the Unclean

Haggai 2:10-14

One of the classic interpretations of history has been reduced to three words: "History repeats itself." This is the cyclic view. There seems to be a sense, at least, in which this is true. Anyone familiar with the ingenious, energetic, imaginative reclamation of Palestine, going on now since 1948, will likely remark to himself that here is one instance in which history is repeating itself. The student of Bible history knows that this modern effort is not the first time the Jewish people have rebuilt their country. It has been done before.

Haggai lived right in the middle of such a time. In fact, had Haggai not lived, it is quite possible the reconstruction project of his day might never have come to completion. It is not too much to say of Haggai that he saved the day for his generation.

It was the year 520 B.C. Sixteen years earlier the first contingent of valorous patriots had returned to the site of Judah's former glory, Jerusalem. There was not much to greet them. The walls had been battered down, the Temple stripped and demolished, the houses vandalized and then left to the arsonists. It all added up to a thoroughly disheartening prospect. But with hearts beating high and hopes beating higher, the brave little band fell to the task of rebuilding the city. Their efforts were plagued with

119

heartbreak and disappointment. After sixteen years, the wall stood unfinished; the Temple a gaunt spectre, abandoned and incomplete. Such was Jerusalem when Haggai appeared.

The first task was the Temple. Haggai strengthened the hand of the governor and his people; soon the Temple was built. It could never compare with Solomon's Temple, true, but it was better than nothing. It was the best the straitened times would allow.

Once done, the people sat back to await God's blessings upon them. The Temple, Haggai had insisted, was the touchstone of their relationship to God; it was the symbol of their spiritual attitude. Now it was done; should not the blessings follow?

At this juncture Haggai steps forward with a dramatic play. He calls the priests before the people and asks them to render a decision on a question of the Law.

The question itself is hypothetical, but it casts a long shadow:

If one carries holy flesh in the skirt of his garment, and with his skirt he touches bread, or grain, or wine, or oil, or any meat, is that which the skirt touches holy?

The priests answer, No.

Then comes another question: If one that is unclean because he has touched a dead body, touch bread, or grain, or wine, or oil, or any meat, is that unclean?

And the priests answer, It is unclean (cf. 2:12-13).

This dialogue carries in it two great spiritual principles which speak to modern-day religious life as much as to the day of Haggai. First, goodness is more than a mere formal status; it is a way of life. Second, evil is a power to be reckoned with.

Goodness: A Way of Life

One of the subtlest weapons the devil ever devised was the comforting thought that goodness is nothing more than maintaining good connections. In Haggai's day, that thought was cast with reference to the Temple. The bare syllogism would go something like this:

The Temple is good.

I helped build the Temple.

Therefore, I am good.

In our own day this comfort is cast in reference to the church.

The church is good.

I belong to the church.

Therefore, I am good.

If we can add to that the virtues of attendance and material support, so much the better.

But the question remains for us, as it did in Haggai's Jerusalem, where does it touch us? How much, and in what way does the church make a difference in our lives?

As we move deeper into this decade the evidence points toward a deepening irony. In a September 30, 1964, editorial of the *Baptist Standard* the evidence is quite specific:

A release from the Baptist Press office in Nashville states that church attendance in America has increased by 30 per cent during the last decade and that the total church membership is now 118 million persons. Yet illegitimacy has increased 10 times faster than church membership growth. Venereal disease has increased 72 per cent during the past year. Crime is increasing four times faster than the population. There are now seven million alcoholics in the nation. There are 175,000 more taverns than the combined total of all churches, synagogues, and temples. The American people gamble away more money each year than they spend on religion, medicine, education, and automobiles.

The most tragic fact in the statistics is that a vast number of these who have departed so far from the straight path were once regular in attendance at church, and many of them are still present most [sic] every Sunday. It is good that they have attended services and do, but something is dreadfully wrong when people can sit under the influence of the church's ministry and go right out to seek new ways to sin.[2]

W. E. Sangster, the British Methodist preacher who wrote the book *Love Is Something You Do,* writes somewhere in that book of being present at a great religious celebration in Gloucester where many of the church dignitaries were in attendance. One clergyman on the rostrum was particularly impressive because of his large size, and because of the gorgeous red and black velvet robe he wore. He had a large cross suspended on a chain around his neck. Sangster mentions his horror on noticing that this clergyman, obviously bored at hearing anyone's voice but his own, occupied himself during the principal speaker's address by taking the golden cross from the chain about his neck and using the cross to clean his fingernails.

What Sangster was saying, it seems to me, is that this one act says something about the man. His relationship to the cross that hung about his neck, the gorgeous clerical robes, and all the rest, was only formal and impersonal; it never touched his heart nor transformed his life.

Do you remember the parable our Lord told of the sheep and the goats? (Matt. 25:32-33). The condemnation of the damned came not because they were irreligious, but because their religion made no observable difference.

To them, religious life was a duty to be performed, a detail to be attended to, a formality to be kept intact. When they learned that they were under condemnation, they cried out, "Lord, when saw we thee an hungred, or athirst, or a stranger, or naked, or sick, or in prison, and did not minister unto thee?" Had they only known that this, too, was a part of religious duty, they would have done it. That was their condemnation! There was nothing spontaneous about their religious life; it was all cut and dried. It was a matter of maintaining the Temple and paying the priests.

As important as that is, it is not the sum of religion. The sum of religion for the Christian is to look out on the world in the spirit of Christ, to have the compassion that Christ has, to love those that Christ would love, to take religion out into the marketplace, where it will make a difference that can be noticed.

That is the hope for the church today, even as it was the hope for Jerusalem. Nels Ferre, in *Return to Christianity*, says:

What the world today needs is Christian individuals with depth and power. Such individuals will become the centers of this creative and redeeming fellowship wherever they are. They will become the nuclei of growing and multiplying cells. We need men today whose will to live has been freed from the will to power, to success, to superiority, to social recognition, to possession, and to pretense; and has found its peace and power in the will to love, the will to fellow-ship, the will to self-giving service, the will to do God's will and be His children.

If Haggai could plead his cause with us, I am sure he would remind us that goodness is not merely a formal status; it is a new way of life. For us, it must be the new life in Christ.

Evil to Reckon With

We are very likely to miss the import of the questions Haggai puts to the priests. They involve the ceremonial law of the Jewish faith about which we care little and probably know even less. But perhaps we can make it clear with signs borrowed from algebra. Haggai's question involves that which is clean and unclean. Let the clean be a positive sign $(+)$; the unclean a negative $(-)$.

The first proposition, were we to write it out with these borrowed signs, would read: $+$ and $- = -$. (The positive is overcome by the negative.) His second proposition would read: $-$ and $- = -$. (Two negatives equal a negative.)

Now translated into the language of ethics, Haggai was simply saying that the power of evil is more likely to overcome good than the power of good is likely to overcome evil. In short, evil is a power to be reckoned with.

Would that we knew that early in life! Evil reaches out with a long arm; it casts a shadow far into the future. G. K. Chesterton tells the story that when he was a young student in Cambridge, he overheard some young collegians trying to persuade a friend of theirs to come with them on some devil's errand. Chesterton said he never knew just what it was they wanted the young man to do, but he never forgot the answer that young man made to their proposition: "No, I cannot go," he said. "If I go with you tonight, I shall never again know right from wrong." Chesterton confided that this one remark was the turning point in his own life. But how many of us are aware of the long reach of evil?

> I walked through the woodland meadows, where sweet the thrushes sing,
> And I found on a bed of mosses, a bird with a broken wing;
> I healed its wound, and each morning, it sang its old sweet strain,
> But the bird with the broken pinion never soared as high again.
> I found a young life broken by sin's seductive art;
> And touched with a Christ-like pity, I took him to my heart.
> He lived with a noble purpose and struggled not in vain;
> But the life that sin had stricken never soared as high again.
> But the bird with the broken pinion kept another from the snare;
> And the life that sin had stricken raised another from despair.
> Each loss has its compensation, there is healing for every pain;
> But the bird with the broken pinion never soars as high again.[4]

Evil has a power that reaches in. When the late Archbishop of Canterbury, William Temple, was still a don at Queen's College,

Cambridge, he attended an evangelistic meeting conducted by Dr. Reuben Torrey, to see what the meeting would be like. Upon returning to his rooms in the college, he said to a friend, "Torrey told us that in the dead and dark of night his sins marched past him in scarlet procession. I never feel that way; my sins are gray, all gray."

That is what evil, once done, does to a life; it colors it with grayness, the grayness of death. The apostle Paul saw gray death in himself: "I find then a law, that, when I would do good, evil is present with me. O, wretched man that I am! who shall deliver me from the body of this death?" (Rom. 7:21, 24). The unclean had touched the clean, and all was defiled.

Haggai comes very near to this part of our New Testament in his thought. He saw the deep despair that moral uncleanness brings; he had no remedy to offer. But he was one of the Old Covenant, making minds and hearts ready for the New. Haggai saw that sin abounds; he could not see that grace super-abounds. That came later, in Jesus Christ.

He saw me plunged in deep distress, and flew to my relief;
  For me He bore the painful cross, and carried all my grief,
To Him I owe my life and breath, and all the joys I have;
  He makes me triumph over death, and saves me from the grave.[5]

I read of two homes in Scotland, and in each a daughter had disappointed her parents. One home wrote the girl off as dead and closed the door. The other lighted a candle every night, and in a lonely highland glen that candle said, "Welcome home, lass." One night, soiled and sorry, she came home not knowing what to expect or do; then she saw the candle in the window, its friendly ray piercing the darkness of the night, and offering hope to the grayness of the unclean within.

It was left to Paul to take Haggai's despair and over against its grayness put the bright joy of the new life in Christ. "Who shall deliver me from the body of this death? I thank God through Jesus Christ our Lord. So then with the mind I myself serve the law of God; but with the flesh the law of sin. There is therefore now no condemnation to them which are in Christ Jesus, who walk not after the flesh, but after the Spirit" (Rom. 7:25-8:1).

Notes

1. Cf. *Christianity Today* (July 3, 1961), 25.

2. E. S. James, "The Insufficiency of the Modern Effort," *Baptist Standard* (September 30, 1964), 4.

3. Nels Ferre, *Return to Christianity*.

4. Hezekiah Butterworth, "The Broken Pinion," *Masterpieces . . .*, p. 418.

5. Samuel Stennett, "Majestic Sweetness Sits Enthroned," *Baptist Hymnal* (Nashville: The Broadman Press, 1956), hymn no. 118.

16

Two Losses

Malachi 1:6-8, 2:13-17, 3:13-18

Malachi came upon the scene in the bleak winter of Jerusalem's discontent. The high hopes of the returning exiles had been exhausted in the ninety years since the first little band entered the precincts of the once majestic but now broken city. The glowing predictions of Isaiah, Ezekiel, Zechariah, Jeremiah, and Haggai had long since collapsed, buried by the dust of reality.[1] Jerusalem was now no more than an insignificant desert town, sustained largely by a remembered glory. Economic depression had continued year after year. Crops were poor; parasites had ruined the plants; fruit harvests were disappointing. The priests were corrupt. Grim skepticism prevailed among the people. Even the best were harassed by nagging and persistent doubts.

Accordingly, worship had degenerated into a meaningless form. The people were bringing—and the priests accepting—the halt, the torn, the lame, and the blind for the altar sacrifices. Rivers of tears were being shed, long prayers being prayed, but nothing different was happening. Religion—indeed, life—had become a wearisome thing.

This is when Malachi stepped to the fore. The name Malachi means "my messenger." We might call him "the advocate."

Bravely, this man of God came advocating a deep-seated repentance.

As we read his brief book of fifty-five verses, we detect that the free-swinging style of the earlier prophets is missing. They could take the skeleton of a thought, expose it to the inspiration and challenge of the immediate, and the fired imagination would put flesh on bare bones. But this was not Malachi's method. He was the persuasive advocate, entertaining and rhetorical. Sometimes he was the protagonist. But always he was the messenger, with a fire in his bones, probing and thrusting, seeking to bring down the chill agnosticism that had paralyzed his people.

This messenger of God was concerned that his people had suffered the loss of reverence. They also had suffered the loss of conviction.

Is not that concern relevant to our situation, too?

A Lost Reverence

Malachi built his case carefully, bringing it to a smashing climax. He had the advantage of an audience who knew well the symptoms of which he spoke.

The lost reverence of Malachi's generation centered in a subtle cynicism toward God, a knowing wink when the lore of an innocent and less complicated past day was quoted as a final authority.

Listen to Malachi press his case: "Ye have wearied the Lord with your words. Yet ye say, Wherein have we wearied him? When ye say, Everyone that doeth evil is good in the sight of the Lord, and he delighteth in them; or, Where is the God of judgment?" (2:17).

It is not that Malachi's generation did not have a need for God. No, it was that God seemed to be out of touch, and perhaps, out of date. God was not relevant. What one did, either good or bad, seemed to make no real difference.

This attitude puts the finger on one aspect of the timeless struggle of the life of faith. We joust with this problem in very practical ways.

For instance, we decide that we are going to start off fresh with God. We wipe the slate clean, make resolutions, and push off, running. We are going to attend church more faithfully, give more systematically, witness more intensely. But before long one of the children gets sick, and we have to stay out of church for three Sundays while the sniffles runs its course through the family. The extra cost of the medicine plus the higher heat bills put the family budget in a strain, so we neglect the church offering. We mean to make that up later. While we wrestle with the little nagging guilt feelings that keep nipping at the edges, we suddenly are thrust into that same social situation that has been our undoing so many times before. This time we mean to keep the flags flying at full mast; but almost before we know it, the flag is falling, and we have surrendered—again. Well, just this one last time, but this is definitely and finally the very last!

Then we begin, with certain traces of defensiveness, to take stock. Well now, actually, that little interlude did not make any real difference. The preacher does not know anything about it, and my friends (who would be shocked if they knew) know nothing of it. As far as that church money is concerned, it sure did pull me through a tight spot.

And so the little circle of rationalization narrows, closing out a reverence for God and for the things of God.

Malachi structures into his brief the contention that a lost reverence for God expresses itself in a lost reverence for the altar:

And ye say, Wherein have we polluted thee? In that ye say, The table of the Lord is contemptible. And if ye offer the blind for sacrifice, is it not evil? and if ye offer the lame and sick, is it not evil?

offer it now unto thy governor; will he be pleased with thee, or accept thy person? (1:7-8).

Malachi suggests a startling test here. He asks us to try paying our taxes in the same, haphazard, casual way we put our gifts on the altar. Now that is a test! For the truth is—and it is a hard truth—that a good half or more of every congregation is willing to ride on the other fellow's coattail, a trick which the Federal Government would never allow. A modern David needs to rise and say, "We cannot worship the Lord with that which cost us nothing"—or next to nothing!

But God puts us on our honor.

That is exactly the point Malachi makes. If we have a lost sense of reverence for God, then honor is no point. We can be slipshod, halfhearted, willy-nilly. What difference does it make?

It makes a difference if you really have a reverence for the Heavenly Father.

With sure instinct Malachi singles out another consequence of a lost reverence: the high casualty rate among marriages. At first this may surprise us; what has divorce and remarriage to do with reverence for God?

We need to understand that our attitude toward the marriage altar is colored by our attitude toward the God of the altar. If there is no reverence for the God of the altar, there is no reverence for anything that goes on it, or that goes on around it. Malachi contrasts their free and easy approach toward marriage and the divine intention: the marriage of one man and one woman to each other on a lifetime basis.

Could anything be more timely for us than this? *Tentative* would be a good word to describe the attitude with which most persons approach marriage today. Each of the partners carries to the marriage altar the idea that somewhere there is someone who will spark the magic that marriage is supposed to bring to life.

But when the sparks which fly are not magic, the tentative option is invoked; the marriage is dissolved. Some poor frantic souls of our generation run from the arms of one to the next in an endless quest for happiness which can never quite be overtaken. The sad, anxious quest for that one who will make all the harsh, dreary facts of life fade away goes on endlessly. But alas! such a quest is destined to futility. Marriage is not a free flight into a world of bliss; it is a disciplined attack on the loneliness and insecurity that inheres in life. Only in an irrevocable commitment to one another is there a possibility that two people may work out a relationship of meaning and fulfilment within the framework of marriage. Only such a relationship is worthy of the word "love"; only such love is durable.

> Let me not to the marriage of true minds
> Admit impediments. Love is not love
> Which alters when it alteration finds,
> Or bends with the remover to remove!
> O no! it is an ever-fixed mark,
> That looks on tempests and is never shaken;
> It is the star to every wandering bark,
> Whose worth's unknown, although his height be taken.
> Love's not Time's fool, though rosy lips and cheeks
> Within his bending sickle's compass come;
> Love alters not with his brief hours and weeks,
> But bears it out even to the edge of doom.
> If this be error, and upon me prov'd,
> I never writ, nor no man ever lov'd.
>
> WILLIAM SHAKESPEARE, "Sonnet 116"

Could it be that the loss of reverence for God is at the root of many of our social ills today? Richard Cardinal Cushing has called our national malady an "epidemic of moral anemia," commenting: "The strength of the human character is supported by values, and values are supported by religion, and when any of these falls all of them fall." We are heirs to a strange hodge-

podge of ideas in our generation, and each of them has made
its attack on the idea of reverence. Charles Darwin taught us to
dismiss God from the created order; Sigmund Freud taught us
to dismiss objective morality from the voice of conscience; Ivan
Pavlov taught us to dismiss responsibility from human behavior;
William James taught us to dismiss idealism from human en-
deavor; Karl Marx taught us to dismiss the person from society's
masses; John Dewey taught us to dismiss the functioner from the
function. We may not know these men firsthand and we may
reject their ideas when stated so plainly, yet their influences
have leavened the lump. Our lost reverence for God keeps
cropping out at the altar, in the way we treat our marriage vows,
and in the general drift of society.

Our Lost Conviction

Malachi had one other concern, which in essence, centers in a
loss of conviction. Listen to his graphic description:

And this have ye done again, covering the altar of the Lord with
tears, with weeping, and with crying out, insomuch that he regardeth
not the offering any more, or receiveth it with good will at your
hand (2:13).

Malachi's generation had lost the conviction that sin was
wrong; they required a permanent change. It is never enough
to shed a few tears, make a rededication, and then go back to the
well-worn ruts of indifference and apathy. Listen to the earnest
exhortation of Peter:

For if after they have escaped the pollutions of the world through
the knowledge of the Lord and Saviour Jesus Christ, they are again
entangled therein, and overcome, the latter end is worse with them
than the beginning.
For it had been better for them not to have known the way of

righteousness, than, after they have known it, to turn from the holy commandment delivered unto them.

But it is happened unto them according to the true proverb, The dog is turned to his own vomit again; and the sow that was washed to her wallowing in the mire (2 Pet. 2:20-22).

The second part of this brief on lost conviction is the thought that judgment no longer has any effect. Everything was judged wholly in terms of this life. Said Malachi's contemporaries: "It is vain to serve God: and what profit is it that we have kept his ordinance?"

We would expect the preacher to believe in a final judgment. Perhaps it comes as a surprise to hear a statement from Wernher von Braun, director of the Marshall Space Flight Center, National Aeronautics and Space Administration, confessing belief in a final reckoning:

There are two forces which move us. One is a belief in a Last Judgment when everyone of us has to account for what we did with God's great gift of life on earth. The other is a belief in an immortal soul, a soul which will cherish the award or suffer the penalty decreed in a final judgment. In our modern world people seem to feel that science has somehow made such "religious ideas" untimely or old-fashioned. But I think science has a real surprise for the skeptics. Science, for instance, tells us that nothing in nature, not even the tiniest particle, can disappear without a trace. Nature does not know extinction. All it knows is transformation. Now if God applies this fundamental principle to the most minute and insignificant parts of his universe, does it not make sense to assume that he applies it also to the masterpiece of his creation—the human soul? I think it does. And everything science has taught me—and continues to teach me—strengthens my belief in the continuity of our spiritual existence after death. Nothing disappears without a trace.[2]

A lost reverence for God, a lost conviction of sin and judgment—that is Malachi's brief. In his day, what everyone seemed to have lost, some recovered. In that recovery was their joy.

But the joy of Malachi's converts must be little compared to the joy of Christians. Our gospel is infinitely better. For in our loss of reverence and in our loss of conviction, our central loss is the loss of self. Like the prodigal in the far country, we have lost a sense of identity with the Father. All other losses beside this pale into insignificance. But the story of the prodigal was told by our Lord not to emphasize our lostness; it was to make bold the possibility of our recovery. If we will only come to ourselves and, rising, turn to the Father, we will find a welcome. More, we will find forgiveness. And reverence and conviction. But most of all, we will find our own true selves as sons in the Father's house.

God has set his own candle in the window. Here is a Plus which overcomes our minus, a Clean that overcomes our unclean. John 3:17 puts it this way: "God sent not his Son into the world to condemn the world; but that the world through him might be saved."

Notes

1. Cf. Isaiah 54, Ezekiel 37, Jeremiah 30-31, Zechariah 2, Haggai 2.
2. Wernher von Braun, "Immortality," *This Week* Magazine (January 24, 1960), 2.